BRITAIN
THE LANDSCAPE BELOW

CLB 3264
This edition published in 1993 by Coombe Books.
© 1988 CLB Publishing, Godalming, Surrey, England.
All rights reserved.
Printed and bound in Italy by Milanostampa S.p.A.
ISBN 1 85833 034 3

BRITAIN
THE LANDSCAPE BELOW

Written and Designed by
PHILIP CLUCAS

COOMBE BOOKS

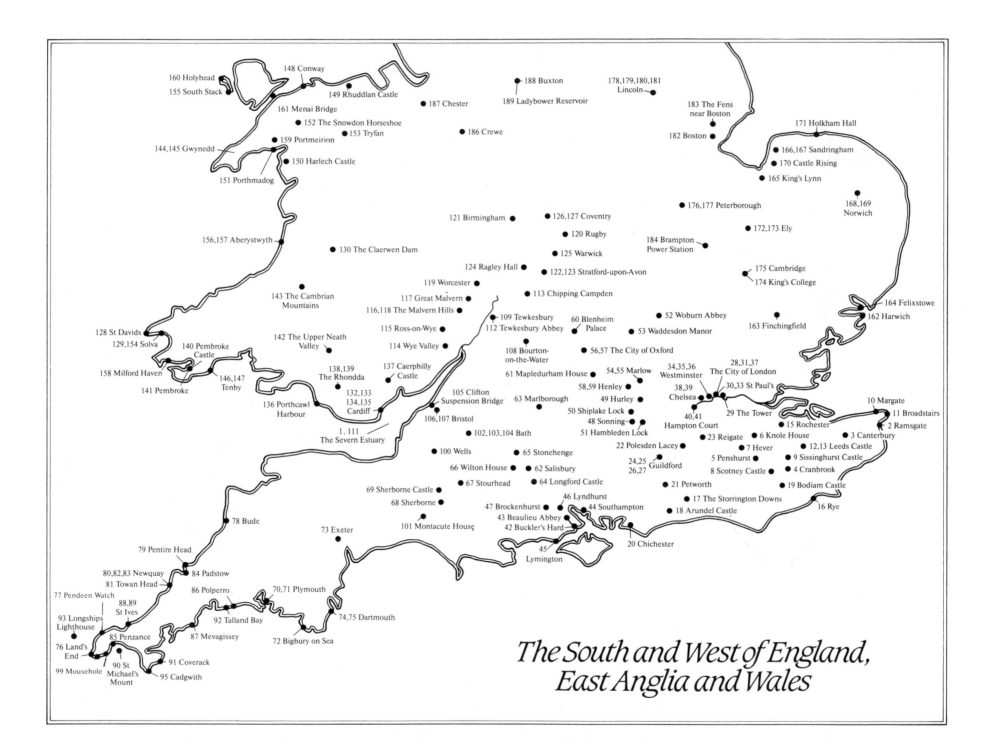

160 Holyhead
155 South Stack
148 Conway
149 Rhuddlan Castle
161 Menai Bridge
152 The Snowdon Horseshoe
153 Tryfan
144,145 Gwynedd
159 Portmeirion
150 Harlech Castle
151 Porthmadog
156,157 Aberystwyth
130 The Claerwen Dam
143 The Cambrian Mountains
128 St Davids
129,154 Solva
140 Pembroke Castle
142 The Upper Neath Valley
158 Milford Haven
146,147 Tenby
141 Pembroke
138,139 The Rhondda
137 Caerphilly Castle
136 Porthcawl Harbour
132,133 134,135 Cardiff
1, 111 The Severn Estuary
78 Bude
79 Pentire Head
80,82,83 Newquay
81 Towan Head
84 Padstow
77 Pendeen Watch
88,89 St Ives
86 Polperro
70,71 Plymouth
93 Longships Lighthouse
92 Talland Bay
74,75 Dartmouth
76 Land's End
85 Penzance
87 Mevagissey
72 Bigbury on Sea
99 Mousehole
90 St Michael's Mount
91 Coverack
95 Cadgwith
73 Exeter
101 Montacute House
69 Sherborne Castle
68 Sherborne
67 Stourhead
66 Wilton House
65 Stonehenge
62 Salisbury
64 Longford Castle
100 Wells
102,103,104 Bath
106,107 Bristol
105 Clifton Suspension Bridge
63 Marlborough
108 Bourton-on-the-Water
61 Mapledurham House
114 Wye Valley
115 Ross-on-Wye
116,118 The Malvern Hills
117 Great Malvern
119 Worcester
113 Chipping Campden
124 Ragley Hall
122,123 Stratford-upon-Avon
125 Warwick
120 Rugby
121 Birmingham
126,127 Coventry
188 Buxton
189 Ladybower Reservoir
187 Chester
186 Crewe
112 Tewkesbury Abbey
109 Tewkesbury
60 Blenheim Palace
52 Woburn Abbey
53 Waddesdon Manor
56,57 The City of Oxford
54,55 Marlow
58,59 Henley
49 Hurley
50 Shiplake Lock
48 Sonning
51 Hambleden Lock
34,35,36 Westminster
28,31,37 The City of London
30,33 St Paul's
38,39 Chelsea
29 The Tower
40,41 Hampton Court
10 Margate
11 Broadstairs
2 Ramsgate
3 Canterbury
15 Rochester
6 Knole House
7 Hever
5 Penshurst
8 Scotney Castle
12,13 Leeds Castle
9 Sissinghurst Castle
4 Cranbrook
23 Reigate
22 Polesden Lacey
24,25 26,27 Guildford
21 Petworth
19 Bodiam Castle
17 The Storrington Downs
16 Rye
18 Arundel Castle
46 Lyndhurst
47 Brockenhurst
44 Southampton
43 Beaulieu Abbey
42 Buckler's Hard
20 Chichester
45 Lymington
184 Brampton Power Station
178,179,180,181 Lincoln
183 The Fens near Boston
171 Holkham Hall
182 Boston
166,167 Sandringham
170 Castle Rising
165 King's Lynn
168,169 Norwich
176,177 Peterborough
172,173 Ely
175 Cambridge
174 King's College
164 Felixstowe
162 Harwich
163 Finchingfield

The South and West of England,
East Anglia and Wales

The natural landscape of the British Isles is astonishingly rich and varied, and the trace of man upon that landscape – in his monuments and in his architecture – is infinitely diverse and splendid. Thus are forged the two features, of nature and of heritage, that make Britain unique among the countries of the world. The past is enshrined in the landscape, and the changes that the British (an amalgam of ancient races – of Celt, Roman, Jute, Angle, Saxon, Norse and Norman) have made upon it. Millennia of geological force and climatic upheaval have shaped the countryside, and centuries of commercial and social interplay have conspired to weave an historical tapestry of great intricacy and colour which is ever present and always awaiting discovery.

Over the length and breadth of Britain there could be no finer way of discovering the land's scenic beauty and appreciating the jewels that mankind has placed therein – be it ancient earthwork, medieval cathedral, bare Gothic abbey or the ruined husks of castles – than to see them from the air. A bird's-eye view offers a vast panorama, at once lyrical and documentary, and much that is too vast to comprehend from the ground can be placed within an all-embracing perspective and seen anew.

The present volume reflects the striking diversity to be found within Britain, and of the 264 specially commissioned photographs included in this, the largest and most lavishly illustrated aerial survey of Britain ever published, each has been selected for the insight that it affords into the natural wonders and architectural glories of these Isles. In the succeeding colour plates and accompanying text the progression through aerial Britain is charted; encompassing all the regions of this enchanted land and, because the undertaking occupied a whole year's duration, the landscape below is to be seen in all the vibrant and varied shades of the seasons.

The journey starts in the South-East, whose tranquil beauties of rolling chalk downland are epitomised by the view of the Storrington Hills *(plate 17)* – enfolded within a cowl of snow, yet dappled with innumerable shades of blue. The area was the invasion coast of old, and along her hilltop trackways came wave after wave of Neolithic farmers and Bronze Age warriors. At a later age, lowland paths rang with the cries of the Legions and, supplanting Rome, came Saxon, Jutish and Anglian families to turn the great wooded valleys of the Weald into fertile expanses of plough and pasture land. The legacies of these ancestral races are to be found in the Chichester *(plate 20)* and Canterbury *(plate 3)* Roman street plans: the

latter's cathedral, under St Augustine and Saxon patronage, developed into the Mother Church of the English nation. The last successful invasion was that of Duke William of Normandy, whose gaunt bastion beside the Medway at Rochester *(plate 15)* speaks volumes about the iron rule of the Norman dynasty. From the 13th to the 15th century the old 'Invasion Coastline' bristled with ragstone castles of England's new 'Defensive Shore'. They number among their finest Bodiam *(plate 19)*, Arundel *(plate 18)* and Leeds Castle *(plates 12 and 13)* – and of the numerous fortified towns walled against the French, the Cinque port of Rye *(plate 16)* in Sussex is one of the most complete. Today, the centuries have cast their spell over them, and they are tinged the colour of honey by time-encrusted lichens – softened at places such as Hever *(plate 7)* and Scotney *(plate 8)* by intimate and 'romantic' gardens, and at Sissinghurst by Tudor knot gardens and wild roses that seemingly ramble at will over the warm red brick of the castle's towering gatehouse *(plate 9)*.

From the counties of Kent, Sussex and Surrey, the progression is to Dunbar's *'Flower of Cities all'* – London – founded through Roman imperialism and massively fortified by the Conqueror's great sentinel of the White Tower at the Tower of London *(plate 29)*; which incorporates bull's blood in its mortar to stand for eternity.

The square mile of the Romano-British capital has developed into the wealthiest square mile on Earth – the City *(plates 28, 31 and 37)*. In the Middle Ages the City was the home of merchants, and the City of Westminster *(plates 35 and 36)* the home of kings. The latter had their abbey church dedicated to St Peter, and the former a cathedral dedicated to St Paul. The cathedral was destroyed in the fire of 1666, and raised again *(plate 30 and 33)* under the guiding genius of Sir Christopher Wren.

From London the way leads westwards, over Wolsey's Thames-side palace, and upstream along the great river as it passes quiet country towns like Marlow *(plates 54 and 55)* and Henley *(plates 58 and 59)*, and snug, unhurried Sonning *(plate 48)* whose beech-laden hills fall precipitously to the water meads below. From here the Thames cuts its meandering course through the chalk-lands of Southern England to the precious architectural gem of Oxford *(plates 56 and 57)*. This line of the Thames was, in ancient times, the northern boundary of Wessex, whence England as a nation was wrested from the grip of Dane. Here, in Hampshire and Wiltshire, are the heartlands of the Kingdom of Alfred, to whom history awards the simple but supreme accolade, *'the Great'*. It was he who built England's first navy –

enabling the modern port of Southampton *(plate 44)* to trace its origins back to the days of the *Anglo-Saxon Chronicle* – and fostering that proud affinity with the sea which filled the ledger at Buckler's Hard *(plate 42)* with orders for merchantmen bound for the Eastern Seas and men o'war for the Navy's deep water fleet.

The Wessex landscape of today is one of bright harvest sunshine, where summer is shrouded in the rich blue of that *'unattainable flower of the sky'*; and the winter scene is one of clouds racing across the countryside, with here and there a gleam of sunlight to flame a blackened hedgerow amber for a few seconds and then to pass onward to where the sun picks out the tower of a church in silver, or the gabled end of a brick-built cottage in military scarlet. Light and shadow everywhere change and exchange upon the chalk scarp of the hills, the evanescent sunshine clarifying small fields without number, whilst into the peace steals the sound of church bells; from the lofty heights of Salisbury's peerless spire *(plate 62)* and from Sherborne's abbey *(plate 68)*; the distant downland hamlets and from New Forest villages such as those at leafy Brockenhurst *(plate 47)* and Lyndhurst *(plate 46)*.

This realm of Alfred – where blood was shed for his dream of England – was ancient long before the Saxons settled here. At least three thousand years earlier, a very different breed of men had grazed their sheep on the hills and tilled the southern fields. Their monuments abound in the countryside still – sarsens, dolmens and megaliths stand in meadow and on bare downs, like human figures frozen for all time, marking the mysterious route to Wiltshire's Neolithic cathedral. More than any other place, Stonehenge *(plate 65)* evokes the darkest and most distant reaches of history.

From the centre of a religion long-lost to the knowledge of man, the western lands of Devon, Cornwall and Somerset – the next visited in this aerial route through Britain – hold a tradition that stretches back to the childhood of Christ Himself. William Blake, when he asked:

> *And did those feet in ancient time,*
> *Walk upon England's mountains green?*
> *And was the Holy Lamb of God*
> *On England's pleasant pastures seen?*
> *And did the Countenance Divine*
> *Shine forth upon our clouded hills?*

was referring to the green landscape of the West. Here also, according to lore, journeyed Joseph of Arimathea, bringing with him the Chalice of the Last Supper – the Holy Grail. It should not be forgotten that the first Christian Church in Britain was never totally destroyed by the heathen invaders, and such soaring monuments as Exeter Cathedral *(plate 73)* and Wells Cathedral *(plate 100)* trace with pride a continuance of worship that stretches back to early Celtic fanes.

It is pleasant to think of the West Country, with its long coastline abutting the surging swell of two seas and the crashing breakers of the open ocean – seen in all its savage splendour at Pendeen Watch *(plate 77)* and Land's End *(plate 76)* – as though it were a country in itself. Indeed,

there is a sense in which it has always been so, for since man first roamed these Isles the Somerset Levels, with their all but impenetrable landscape of marsh and lagoon, have formed a barrier between the lands of Devon and Cornwall and the rest of England. Early lines of communication consisted of tortuous trackways which always followed the highest contour to avoid the steep fall of streams and the area's tidal estuaries. The trails through Somerset and Dorset, where they were low-lying or progressed through forest, were virtually impassable; in some parts of these counties this remained true right up to the advent of the railways. Thus was born the West Countryman's close affinity with the wild-waters of his native coastline (sea-voyage was less fraught with hazard than overland travel), forging that proud kinship with the sea displayed at ports such as Dartmouth *(plates 74 and 75)* and Plymouth *(plates 70 and 71)* – forever evocative of Elizabeth's reign, when it held the destiny of the English Realm. There are scores of tiny fishing villages such as Polperro *(plate 86)*, Padstow *(plate 84)*, Mevagissey *(plate 87)*, Coverack *(plate 91)* and Cadgwith *(plate 95)* which nestle beside harsh granite cliffs overlooking the broad surges of the bar and the everlasting thunder of the long Atlantic swell.

The Bristol Channel *(plates 1 and 111)* leads the way northeastwards – past the greatest of ancient ports, Bristol *(plates 106 and 107)*, whose graceful neighbour Bath *(plate 102 to 104)*, has been acclaimed the most elegant of all British cities – to view the lands of the River Wye *(plate 114)* at Ross-on-Wye *(plate 115)*; and to delve into the rolling landscape of the Severn and Avon Valleys. Here are found elm-fringed meadows, and orchards laden with damson, cherry, apple and pear. It is the verdant heartland of England *(plates 122 and 123)*, so beloved of Shakespeare; the misty-green vale from which Elgar drew his music and, centuries beforehand, Langland his vision of *'Piers Plowman'*. The land is naturally at its most beautiful at Eastertide, when its orchards are enveloped in a white foam of blossom. In pockets of wayside vegetation bluebells are found in such profusion that coppice-margins and hedgebanks are *'washed wet like lakes'* bathed in pools of light – whose sheen continually changes as the drooping flower heads swirl in heavily-scented breezes. Above the beauties of the Severn rise the medieval Abbey of Tewkesbury *(plates 109 and 112)* and the Cathedral tower at Worcester *(plate 119)*; their construction meticulously honed to complement the countryside's unique qualities of light – an effect best observed (in the words of Langland's poetry), *'In a somer seson when soft was the sonne'*. Indeed, it is this element of luminosity – of gathering light – that best characterises the jagged Malvern Hills *(plates 116 and 118)* to the west, and illumines the gentle, bow-headed landscape of the Cotswolds which stretch beyond the vale to south and to east. It is here, in towns such as Bourton-on-the-Water *(plate 108)* and Chipping Campden *(plate 113)* with their predominance of honey-brown masonry, that the stones themselves appear to glow.

Travelling westwards again, the exhilarating vistas of Wales are encountered in the ancient southern Principality of Deheubarth, where a chain of English Marcher castles stretch from the Forest of Dean to St David's Cathedral *(plate 128)* on Dyfed's Atlantic headland. They number, among their finest, Caerphilly Castle *(plate 137)*, Carew, Chepstow and Pembroke *(plates 140 and 141)*, whose towns grew up beneath their Norman walls; quiet places nowadays that seem to belong to their past, half asleep in the shadow of their castle crags. Thus, through great medieval upheavals – the crumbling power of the Llewellyn princes; the encroachment of Marcher fiefs; the campaigns in northern Wales of the Plantagenet kings, who built fortresses at Conway *(plate 148)* Rhuddlan *(plate 149)* and Harlech *(plate 150)*; and the culminating tragedy of Owain Glyndwr – has the flower of Celtic independence retreated; seemingly into the mountainous fastness of the surrounding countryside.

Wales is an extraordinary mixture of the obvious and the recondite, a country of romantic legends and shattered bastions. Yet the overpowering spirit of the landscape is one of Gothic drama – a wild, mountainous terrain of vast, indigo, cloud-misted distances, pervaded by the sound of sweet-water and birdsong. Here is a depth of vision leading into the centre of an almost untouchable world of clear light, moorland and lovely valleys – as exemplified by the Upper Neath Valley *(plate 142)*, the Rheidol Vale *(plate 131)* and at the Claerwen Dam *(plate 130)*. However, soaring above all, dominating all, are the mountains – of the Cambrian Range *(plate 143)*, of Tryfan *(plate 153)*, and of a host of others – yet it is to the ethereal, azure mass of Snowdon *(plate 152)* that the focus of bardic song and sentiment has turned throughout the ages.

From the ancient savagery and power of the West's moors, mountains and seascapes, we next cross the country to the relatively flat lands of East Anglia – where the landscape is typically one of sweeping views in low relief. It comprises areas of Fenlands, whose dark waters cowl sedge-swamps and reed-beds in shadowed morasses; of estuary; mile upon mile of mud flats, and *'meals'* – vast sand dunes – a lonely kingdom of wildfowl, where wading birds and geese flock in their thousands. However, in direct contrast to these desolate spots where nature is racked by piercing winds driven inland from the North Sea, the majority of the eastern counties is given over to intensive arable farming – such as that which surrounds the village of Finchingfield *(plate 163)* in Essex – whose rich, dark soils are numbered among the most fertile in the world. Here the landscape is entirely pastoral, swelling into gentle, golden ridges, the crests of which carry hedgerows, occasional coppice woodland and, in the vales, stream-splashed water meads and farmsteads which, in the Middle Ages, supplied the wool that gave rise to the trading ports of Boston *(plate 182)* and King's Lynn *(plate 165)*; and supplied the wealth that prospered the great cathedral cities of Lincoln *(plates 178 and 181)*, Norwich *(plates 168 and 169)*, Peterborough *(plates 176 and 177)* and Ely *(plates 172 and 173)*, whose Norman towers and peerless octagon stand out defiantly against the violent light of the endless flats of the Great Level – representing the finest flower of medieval architecture.

From the Fenland of the Wash, and the Wolds of Lincolnshire, the journey is northwards to the ancient Saxon Kingdom of Northumbria and the wild, often windswept counties which share a history as turbulent as any in Britain. Warkworth *(plate 201)* and Bamburgh *(plate 196)* are

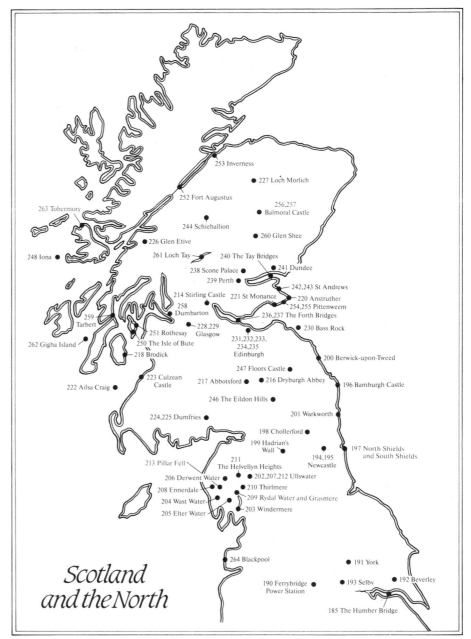

Scotland and the North

eloquent testimony to the bloodshed and conflict of the past; yet it is the Roman Wall *(plate 199)* which, more than anything else, speaks of its own rueful strength of purpose.

In the days before industrialisation laid wide-grasping hands upon the valleys and rivers, there was scarcely a square mile of land lying between the waters of the Humber and the Tweed which had not some charm and beauty to reveal. But when the demand for iron-ore and coal increased – the latter now feeding power stations such as Ferrybridge *(plate 190)* and Brampton *(plate 184)* – stretches of hitherto solitary land became utterly changed in aspect and character. Fortunately the major part of the northern landscape remains unscarred and still forms one of the largest tracts of unspoilt countryside in England. The Peak country of Derbyshire continues to be an expanse of loveliness – especially around the spa town of Buxton *(plates 188 and 189)*. The Lakelands of Cumbria *(plates 202 to 213)* still hold the souls of their poets, and the great Yorkshire Dales remain unspoilt, shading with solitude the *'bare ruined choirs'* of shattered Fountains Abbey, Bolton Priory and Rievaulx. The very remoteness of their setting – which nowadays makes them so 'romantically sited' – is also their tragedy, for when the monasteries were disbanded in the 16th century there were no parishioners of any nearby town to save the buildings. All honour therefore, to the citizens of Beverley *(plate 192)* and Selby *(plate 193)* who, more than four hundred years ago, had the courage and good sense to buy their monastic churches from the Crown for parochial use. Selby Abbey is built in white magnesian limestone – as encountered at York Minster *(plate 191)* – and today shines like a beacon in the centre of what is otherwise an undistinguished town.

In Northumbria the Pennines merge imperceptibly with the Cheviot Hills, whose remote summits command inspiring views of the River Tweed gliding away to Berwick *(plate 200)* and the far sea. These hills, which once resounded to the clash of sword and claymore in the fierce hand-to-hand fighting of the Border Wars, now echo only to the cry of the curlew. In summer they 'shade fair' with eglantine and hairbell, and the prevailing colour of the land is stained with the purple of heather and the yellow of vast swags of gorse and broom. Yet in winter's grip – if the moors have not become interfolded acres of drifting snow and hazy blue shadow – the colour of the land takes on a sinister hue, reflecting the predominant granite rocks in bleak greyness, or in the browns of dead bracken. Amid such scenery – where star saxifrage and spring gentians are still to be found – the bold domes of the Cheviots ride across the Scottish border like massive waves. These lands are confusingly called the Lowlands – a description which might suggest flatness and a certain lack of variety, yet nothing could be further from the truth. The Scottish Lowlands – a tableland of grassy hills and cool green pasture that gives shelter to ruined Dryburgh Abbey *(plate 216)*, Culzean Castle *(plate 223)*, and Sir Walter Scott's home at Abbotsford *(plate 217)* – stand in dignity, possessing a loveliness that is apt to be overlooked in comparison with the more dramatic splendours that the rugged northwestern Highlands provide. Yet these Lowlands are more hilly than most parts of England, and the climate, particularly in the central area, can be as harsh in mid-winter – when the first flurries of snow come scudding over the summits of the Tweedsmuir, Lammermuir and Pentland Hills – as that endured by any lonely hamlet in the Highland mountains. Along the line of cliffs at the shore are found fine, old fishing villages – at Brodick *(plate 218)*, Anstruther *(plate 220)*, St Monance *(plate 221)* and Pittenweem *(plates 254 and 255)* – which are backed by agricultural land where the traditional white walls of the Scottish farmsteads make a delicious splash against the monotone of pasture and land under plough.

Coming up country from the border, through a land of grey stone and rounded hills, dotted with romantic ruins of long ago – bare skeletons of broken priories and slighted castles – may be seen the jagged frieze of the Highlands (the last stage in the progression through the landscape below) which rise above the northern horizon; blue and dramatic and unmistakable. Here are found Schiehallion *(plate 244)*, the Trossachs, the Monadhliaths, Glen Shee *(plate 260)*, the Cairngorms and the isolated mountains of the far north, whose capacity – perhaps an effect of atmospherics – to take on at a distance a wistful, cerulean blue, characterizes all the great mountains of the Heights. These awesome ranges share the landscape with wild kyles and sea lochs that endlessly stud the region and gouge deeply into the land; with icy streams that tumble through green and wooded glens; with frowning crags and darkly shadowed passes; with the calm waters of vast inland lochs – such as Loch Tay *(plate 261)* and Loch Ness *(plate 252)* – and the western seaboard's myriad islands; of Gigha *(plate 262)*, of Ailsa Craig *(plate 222)* and of Columba's sacred Iona *(plate 248)*. Yet above all, it is the ever-changing sky that characterises Highland Scotland and gives rise to an immense variety of shade and subtle hue.

The Severn Estuary in the luminous glow of sunrise **(plate 1)** imparts an urgent sense of the mystery which this commanding seascape demands. It is a place of rushing tides and dangerous currents; and it is not surprising that the Celtic god of the estuary, *Noadu*, survived the Roman occupation, worshipped under the new title *Nodeus*. On Romano-British ornaments she is represented mounted on a seahorse, riding majestically on the crest of the Severn bore.

BRITAIN
THE LANDSCAPE
BELOW

CLB 3264
This edition published in 1993 by Coombe Books.
© 1988 CLB Publishing, Godalming, Surrey, England.
All rights reserved.
Printed and bound in Italy by Milanostampa S.p.A.
ISBN 1 85833 034 3

The medieval richness of **Canterbury (plate 3)** is summarised in the soaring stateliness of the cathedral, whose architecture, from Norman to Perpendicular, is magnificent, and whose 13th-century stained glass is the equal of Bourges and Chartres. On a lesser scale, but with no less pride and piety, the golden sandstone church of **Cranbrook (plate 4)** was raised during the zenith of the cloth-trade, towards the end of the 15th century. As with Henry Dobell's smock windmill of 1814, the medieval church of St Dunstan's still expresses the prosperity of long-dead industries; and the unmistakable air which the Wealden town acquired through commercial success. Another Wealden village, that of **Penshurst (plate 5)** possesses a Renaissance palace, glorified by the enduring legend of the Elizabethan courtier Sir Philip Sidney, where a half-remembered story of heroic self-denial draws thousands of 'pilgrims' to Penshurst Place each year. The Tudor palace does not dominate the village as it might, but sits discreetly behind the main street, to be seen on entering or leaving the village, yet never obtruding on the scene of modest old houses, an inn and well-proportioned church.

Ramsgate (plate 2) was a fishing village which grew into a Regency resort. In the last century it was greatly enlarged and architecturally there are good things for the admirer of Victoriana, including a church designed by, and the burial place of, Augustus Pugin.

(Overleaf: plates 4 and 5)

Perhaps the finest of all Kent's great houses is at **Knole (plate 6)** in Sevenoaks, where massed vaults of masonry resemble a small town rather than a house. It was originally an arch-bishop's palace, but it passed to the Sackville family through the gift of Queen Elizabeth I. **Hever Castle (plate 7)**, some ten miles distant from Knole, is also associated with the Virgin Queen, for it was here that her father, Henry VIII, patiently courted and eventually won the hand of her ill-fated mother, Anne. The Tudor brick of **Sissinghurst Castle (plate 9)** has mellowed to a rich, purplish red, and its confused tangle of buildings, with an unusually tall gatehouse, forms a fine backdrop for the gardens created by Victoria Sackville-West. It was she, and her husband Sir Harold Nicolson, who restored the once great manor house and established it as one of the finest gardens in the country – much of it laid out in Elizabethan style. Of especial interest is the white garden, planted entirely with silver-leaved white flowering species, separated by box hedges.

At **Scotney Castle (plate 8)** also, there is to be found the happy combination of a landscape of great natural beauty, historic interest, and the rarest harmony of buildings, trees and flowers. The new house, built by Antony Salvin in 1837, has terraces of rhododendrons and azaleas which fall sharply away to the almost unbearably picturesque vista of medieval castle ruins rising from the crystal waters of a lily-covered lake.

(Overleaf: plates 8 and 9)

Although **Broadstairs (plate 11)** has claims to antiquity, it is to **Margate (plate 10)** that the accolade of oldest and most famous resort in Kent must be given. Here, it is claimed, the English habit of seaside holidays was born. A Margate man invented the bathing machine – so beloved of George III that he sponsored the Royal Sea Bathing Hospital.

A list of dignitaries who came for the bathing and the Thanet air would indeed be impressive. Today, alas, the resort has lost much of its Regency character – swept away beneath a tide of tourism.

■ **Leeds Castle (plates 12 and 13)**, a medieval stronghold with later additions, is a superbly sited fortification built on two islands in a lake created by the damming of the River Len. The first is natural, and reached by a bridge through a fine Edwardian gatehouse leading to a walled bailey, at the far end of which is a castellated house. Beyond is a small building, the *Gloriette*, rising out of the waters to form a small artificial island.

(Overleaf: plates 12 and 13)

The **River Medway (plate 14)** winds through the county of Kent, touching the town of Tonbridge and Maidstone, but for most of its course its muddy waters – overhung by hazel and alder – are fringed by lush countryside. Just before the river meets and mingles with the creeks and salt flats of the Thames Estuary lies the town of **Rochester (plate 15)**. Its position is strategically of the first importance. There has been a bridge at Rochester across the Medway from earliest times, and it was an important Roman town on the great road from Dover to London; here too the Normans built one of their most powerful castles, second only in priority and scale to the Tower of London. The castle was begun under the direction of Bishop Gundulf, the most famous of all the Norman military architects, but the keep, which rises 130ft above the grass of the bailey, was built in Henry I's reign. Following the practice of the time there was no entrance at ground level; entry had to be made at first-floor level through a square forebuilding. The enormously thick walls of the battlements command the most comprehensive view of the cathedral church at Rochester (the second oldest diocese in the country) which rises in the arc of the castle's shadow. With a decline in military status came prosperity of a different kind, and a number of substantial houses are witness to the wealth and pride of Rochester's merchants in the 16th and 17th centuries.

Of all England's counties **Sussex is the easiest to visualise.** It lies more or less in four parallel strips, the northern boundary being forest, the next strip the clay weald, then comes the smooth, green line of the Downs – whose rolling, whale-back quality is exemplified at **Storrington (plate 17)** where it recalls Kipling's sentiments: *'bare slopes where chasing shadows skim, And through the gaps revealed Belt upon belt, the wooded, dim, Blue goodness of the weald'.* The final zone comprises the coastline of chalk cliff and low-lying plain.

The streams that flow from the South Downs, though small, have historic import. **Rye (plate 16)**, one of the old Cinque Ports , at one time stood at the mouth of its stream, but now, owing to the receding sea, finds itself inland. Here in medieval times the waves lapped at the very foot of the Ypres Tower, yet now the tide breaks some two miles to the south. **Arundel Castle (plate 18)**, beside the Arun, was built to defend the break made by that river through the chalky soil of the Downs.

At **Bodiam (plate 19)**, a special licence from the Crown enabled Sir Edward Dalyngrigge to build, in 1385, one of the last of the genuine medieval castles, to protect his estate from the incursions of the French. The moat, which is fed by a tributary stream of the River Rother, is still well filled, and together with the gatehouse, walls and drum-towers at the angles, forms one of the most beautiful and evocative castle ruins in Britain.

(Overleaf: plates 18 and 19)

Chichester (plate 20), the county town of West Sussex, was known to the Romans as *Noviomagus* and their town layout, of four main streets enclosed by a wall, still exists.

Chichester is chiefly noted for its Georgian architecture, its fine town houses and cruciform cathedral. The latter is substantially the church erected over eight hundred years ago by Ralph Luffa, Bishop from 1091 until 1123. The detached bell tower of the mid-15th century stands beside the Great West Front and is the only such example of cathedral architecture to be found in England.

■ **Petworth (plate 21)** boasts many 16th and 17th-century houses, which include among their number Thompson's Almshouses of 1618 and Somerset Lodge which is thirty years its junior. Of their number, Petworth House is the town's principal treasure – being a magnificent 17th and 19th-century mansion sited a little to the west of St Mary's church. The boundary walls of the great park in which the mansion stands extend into the town itself.

A light scattering of snow serves to highlight the formal elegance of **Polesden Lacey (plate 22)**, set in a Surrey landscape once described as *'though deep, yet clear; though gentle, yet not dull; strong without rage; without o'erflowing, full'*. In such terrain, amid Surrey's timbered cottages and Victorian villas with their well-tended gardens, are scattered the county's handful of old and precious towns – Guildford, Dorking, Farnham, Bletchingley and **Reigate (plate 23)**. The latter, although not mentioned by name until the 12th century, was a manor of the powerful de Warenne family, Earls of Surrey in the reign of William the Conqueror. Here they built a strongly fortified castle where, according to legend, the barons deliberated before their encounter with King John at Runnymede and the signing of the *Magna Carta*. Sadly nothing now remains of Reigate's castle, save for the mound on which it once stood, whose dry fosse and traces of moat are well picked out by the effects of snow, low winter shadow and the aerial perspective.

Guildford (plates 24, 25, 26 and 27), in Surrey, is a town of ancient lineage sited on the River Wey. It was here that the medieval Pilgrims' Way, which led from Winchester to the 'Shrine of the Holy Martyr' at Canterbury (following the prehistoric track along the Downs) forded the river. Settlement was first mentioned in the reign of Alfred the Great, and in the Middle Ages the town found favour with a number of monarchs who built palaces and a great castle here. The town flourished as an important centre of the wool trade, and although nothing now remains of its royal residences – save for the castle's three-storied keep *(plate 25, centre)* – the prosperity of the wool trade had an abiding influence over Guildford's architecture.

The town's 'old world' character is contrasted by modern development; in particular by the striking and controversial new buildings of the University of Surrey and Sir Edward Maufe's new, brick-built cathedral *(plate 24)* which crowns the summit of Stag Hill.

(Overleaf: plates 26 and 27)

On the north bank of the grey ribbon of the Thames, which threads its course past sprawling Victorian wharves **(plate 32),** stands London's medieval heart, which now constitutes that richest part of the capital known simply as **'The City' (plates 28 and 31).** The mercantile square mile has at its centre Wren's Classical masterpiece, **St Paul's Cathedral (plates 30 and 33),**

which rose like a phoenix from the ashes of the Great Fire of London to dominate the Stuart capital. Today's 'temples of mammon', in the form of unfortunate and ill-conceived glass towers **(plate 37)** poke their intrusive heads above the City's stone and concrete jungle, yet for all they attain in height they fail to overshadow Wren's glorious dome.

On the City's eastern boundary stands the dizzy prospect of **'Her Majesty's Tower of London' (plate 29)** – a grey, uneven maze, harsh in the texture of its stone, rugged with crenellations and dark with sinister association.

(Previous pages: plates 28 and 29)

The enormous, twin glass roofs of **Victoria Railway Station (plate 34, centre)** span a concourse teeming with commuters from the southern Home Counties and from Brighton (which is but an hour's journey away). Within five minutes walk of the rush-hour *maelstrom* may be found peaceful haunts of solitude in the silence of St James's Park and Green Park whose tree-filled acres spread to surround the honeyed stone of Buckingham Palace, the residence of sovereigns since the reign of George II, and once described by Pepys as *'a country house in summer, and a town house in winter'*.

From the leafy seclusion of St James's, southeast across Whitehall, the eye scans the architecture of England at the height of Empire until it is arrested by the enormous neo-Gothic form of the **Palace of Westminster (plates 35 and 36)**, standing cheek by jowl with Westminster Hall. The latter was originally raised by William Rufus and altered by Richard II, who feasted ten thousand of London's poor there daily during the Christmastide of 1398. Westminster Hall has since been the scene of some of the most famous trials in England's history.

Opposite the Red King's Hall is Westminster Abbey, London's one entirely beautiful possession. Built originally by the saintly Edward the Confessor, it was massively and elaborately enlarged by Henry III. This *'short, stout and ungainly old man with a blinking left eye'* has here left to us, by his munificence and foresight, a promise of permanence in a world of change.

(Previous pages: plates 32 and 33. Overleaf: plates 36 and 37)

At **Chelsea (plate 38)** the pace
of the City and Westminster is
replaced by an atmosphere of
calm – born of shady, tree-
lined streets, abounding in
antiquities and memories of
great men. For centuries the
area has been secluded from
the spread of London by
the natural barrier of creeks
running north from the Thames
– where now stands Victoria
Station – and by the marshy
area of the Five Fields. It is
here, on the northern river
shore, that the grand set-
piece of Chelsea architecture
stands – the **Royal Hospital
(plate 39)**, set back behind
its flanks of trees and sweep
of lawn, with a long, chaste
front and an austere pillared
portico between two projecting
wings of dark, mellow brick
touched at the quoins with
Portland stone. It has a
superb modesty of fitness of
place and purpose – as Carlyle
grudgingly noted *'quiet and
dignified and the work of a
gentleman'*. The gentleman
involved was Sir Christopher
Wren, who, at the behest of
its instigator Charles II,
built it to be used as a
hospital for aged or disabled
soldiers.

Also raised in brick (and
among the first of the genre)
is Wolsey's great palace of
**Hampton Court (plates 40
and 41)**. Yet, despite the
influence of its great
founder, it is Henry VIII
whose image seems indelibly
stamped upon the place. The
view from the air reveals the
overwhelming vastness of the
various ranges of buildings,
and the formal splendour of
the palace gardens – the
tiltyard, the maze, the
fountain garden, the sunken
arbours, the knot garden and
the meticulously planned and
planted 'wilderness'.

(Overleaf: plates 40 and 41)

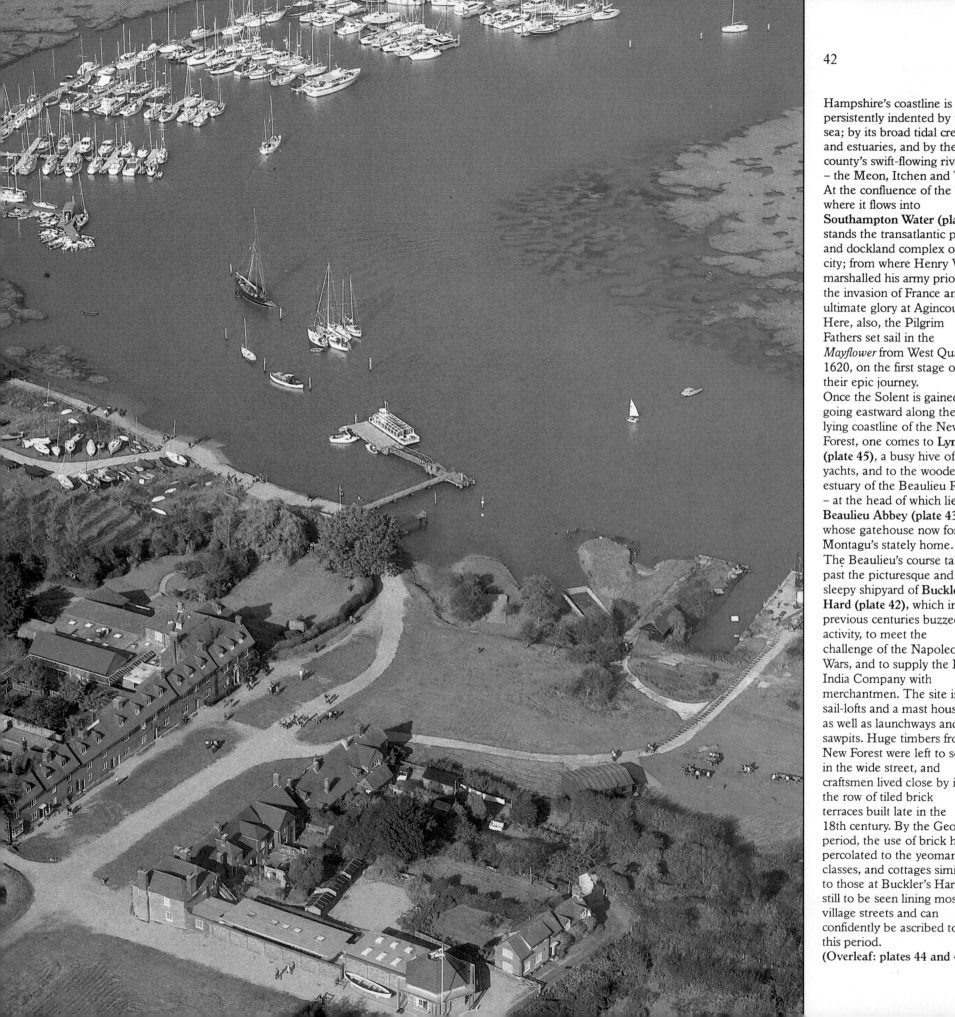

Hampshire's coastline is persistently indented by the sea; by its broad tidal creeks and estuaries, and by the county's swift-flowing rivers – the Meon, Itchen and Test. At the confluence of the Test, where it flows into **Southampton Water (plate 44)**, stands the transatlantic port and dockland complex of the city; from where Henry V marshalled his army prior to the invasion of France and ultimate glory at Agincourt. Here, also, the Pilgrim Fathers set sail in the *Mayflower* from West Quay in 1620, on the first stage of their epic journey.

Once the Solent is gained, going eastward along the low-lying coastline of the New Forest, one comes to **Lymington (plate 45)**, a busy hive of yachts, and to the wooded estuary of the Beaulieu River – at the head of which lies **Beaulieu Abbey (plate 43)**, whose gatehouse now forms Lord Montagu's stately home. The Beaulieu's course takes it past the picturesque and sleepy shipyard of **Buckler's Hard (plate 42)**, which in previous centuries buzzed with activity, to meet the challenge of the Napoleonic Wars, and to supply the East India Company with merchantmen. The site included sail-lofts and a mast house, as well as launchways and sawpits. Huge timbers from the New Forest were left to season in the wide street, and craftsmen lived close by in the row of tiled brick terraces built late in the 18th century. By the Georgian period, the use of brick had percolated to the yeoman classes, and cottages similar to those at Buckler's Hard are still to be seen lining most village streets and can confidently be ascribed to this period.

(Overleaf: plates 44 and 45)

The New Forest, created by William the Conqueror in
1079 as an enormous hunting park, covers the whole of
the beheaded triangle of Hampshire enclosed by the
rivers Blackwater and Avon, the Channel and
Southampton Water. It is not, as one might suppose, an
unbroken tract of woodland, but the area's fascination is
in its richness of variety. Here we have open parkland,
stretches of bracken, heather hummocks glowing pink in
summer, and noble avenues of stately trees.
Clustered within this land of variation – where wild
ponies graze and roam at will through oak-fringed glades
where kings once hunted – are the woodland-lapped
villages of **Brockenhurst (plate 47)** and **Lyndhurst
(plate 46)** the capital of the New Forest. The former has
a fine church of Norman origin which claims to be the
oldest foundation in the forest. Brockenhurst is
principally renowned, however, for the grave of Brusher
Mills, the famous New Forest snakecatcher responsible
for the demise of over three thousand adders.

(Overleaf: plates 48 and 49)

To the north of Hampshire lies the quiet, unpretentious countryside of Berkshire, little concerned with outside approbation and making no effort to popularise its charms or to advertise its wistful beauty. It is enfolded in hill and dell, like the roll of the sea's swell; a pleasantly undulating land of cottage-like churches with wooden belfries, thatched timber barns and cob-houses, farmland hamlets and small, red-brick towns.

The Thames forms the county's northern border and here there are orchards extending for several miles to the south until the Downs are reached. At **Sonning (plate 48)**, a lovely riverside village with an old mill and an eleven-arch bridge (one of the oldest spanning the Thames), the beech woods of the heights descend to the river's bank. Downstream, at nearby **Hurley (plate 49)** the Thames splits to form islands which, together with some charming backwaters, makes this unspoilt reach of the river particularly attractive. Between the two lie **Hambleden Lock (plate 51)**, and **Shiplake Lock (plate 50)** near the village of Wargrave – itself surrounded by towering elms and set in one of the three ancient clearings of the Windsor Forest which, at the time of Edward the Confessor, supported pannage for one hundred pigs and land for several ploughs.

(Overleaf: plates 52 and 53)

Marlow (plates 54 and 55) in Buckinghamshire is a fascinating riverside town which has much to recommend it in its mixture of old and new. It is planned in such a way that none of the modern buildings detract from the charm of the older ones. The High Street runs at a right angle to the Thames, which is crossed by Marlow's most famous feature – its suspension bridge built in 1829 to the design of William Tierney Clark. On its northern flank the church of St Peter preserves an object said to be the mummified hand of St James the Apostle – brought here in the 16th century from Reading Abbey.

The very movement to dissolve the monasteries, which led to the suppression of Reading Abbey, fostered the development of the English country house as we know it today; for most of the landed estates include former ecclesiastic property redistributed to Henry VIII's supporters, and countless country houses in England owe their character as well as their names to earlier religious foundations on the same site. Indeed, the courtyard plans of some great classical houses – such as **Woburn Abbey (plate 52)** – hark back to long-vanished cloisters.

Waddesdon Manor (plate 53) is a vast, spreading country mansion of French Renaissance style set in one hundred and sixty acres of parkland, built by the architect Gabriel Hippolyte Destailleur for Baron de Rothschild in 1877-89. The gardens were laid out at the same time by another Frenchman, Laine .

(Overleaf: plates 56 and 57)

Oxfordshire is the county for the lover of noble architecture. Its churches stand out as the finest among the shires. Its manor houses, too, represent every style of architecture, from Vanburgh's monumental **Blenheim Palace (plate 60)** to the gentle Elizabethan brick of **Mapledurham House (plate 61)**; the inspiration for Grahame's 'Toad Hall'.

Henley (plates 58 and 59) is also set in the beautiful wooded countryside of the Thames Valley, yet it is to the **City of Oxford (plates 56 and 57)** that the eye turns for the supreme delights of architecture. Here, among a forest of *'dreaming spires and pinnacles'*, is breathtaking beauty – in the unsurpassed, broad sweep of the 'High', past Magdalen College and Queen's College on the one

hand, and University College on the other. From Carfax, where four roads meet, it is but a stone's throw to Tom Tower; the entrance to Christ Church with its Cathedral; the gardens of St John's and the big quad at Balliol.

(Overleaf: plates 60 and 61)

Upon the bare scarp of the Wiltshire Plain a low sun and harsh shadows dramatise the huge megaliths of **Stonehenge (plate 65)**. An aerial view wonderfully reveals the encircling ditch and bank that date from the Stone Age – upon which the stupendous Bronze Age temple was later developed into circles of sarsen stones around a horseshoe of trilithons enclosing the enigmatic Welsh bluestones. To the south, in the Valley of Avon, the cathedral city of **Salisbury (plate 62)** is almost encircled by the vastness of the downs, so that from whatever direction it is approached, the tall, captivating spire (at 404ft the tallest of any cathedral in Britain) provides the first intimation of the city. Indeed, Salisbury has no history earlier than its cathedral, for both were planned upon a virgin site in the water-meads of the Avon, when the hilltop town of Old Sarum was abandoned during the 13th century.

One of the most magnificent tombs within the cathedral is that of Sir Thomas Gorges and his wife, Helena. It is they who, in 1573, commenced the building of the romantic castle at **Longford (plate 64)** a few miles downstream from Salisbury. The peculiar design is based upon the shield of the Holy Trinity, and the cost of its construction almost ruined Sir Thomas. However, when a Spanish galleon was wrecked while he was Governor of Hurst Castle, his wife begged the hull from Queen Elizabeth. The ship was later discovered to be full of silver bars, and with this fortune Longford Castle was completed in 1591.

Plate 63: the elegant market town of **Marlborough**.

(Overleaf: plates 64 and 65)

At **Wilton House (plate 66)** and, more especially, at **Stourhead (plate 67)** – both in Wiltshire – the English landscape gardens of the early 18th century were invented. Their abiding spirit is the most poetic of all the dreams of antiquity, the most transporting evocation in the living form of nature of Claude and Poussin's two-dimensional art. The great picture

garden was begun at Wilton by the 9th Earl of Pembroke, whose elegant Palladian bridge spans the River Nadder; and at Stourhead by Henry Hoare in 1740.

Stourhead is the first of the completely informal landscape compositions which were the special English contribution to the art of gardening. At the centre of

Stourhead's three-armed lake, the Doric Temple of Flora reflects its Tuscan portico in the smooth waters at its feet, and nearby can be seen the Pantheon, shining against its luxuriant, wooded background. High above the surface of the lake, amid dense trees, is seen the circular Temple of the Sun, after the original at Baalbek.

Sherborne (plate 68), the most beautiful and architecturally constant of all Dorset towns, lies in one of the many shallow valleys of the tributaries of the upper Stour. Its greatest pride is its yellow-stone abbey church, raised by the Norman architect and minister to Henry I, Roger de Caen. To the immediate north of the abbey, and occupying a major part of the dissolved monastery building, is Sherborne's famous boys' school, founded in 1550.

Just east of the town are two castles, known locally as the Old and New; the one very ruinous and the other a stately home built c1594 by Sir Walter Raleigh. The latter, **Sherborne Castle (plate 69),** faces its predecessor across a wide expanse of water; an artificial lake created in the 18th century by Capability Brown. It was here, at Sherborne Castle (so legend tells), that Raleigh, while smoking tobacco he had brought back from Virginia, was doused with beer by his servant who thought he was on fire.

(Overleaf: plates 70 and 71)

Devon and the sea are inextricably linked, and her sons have for centuries braved the treacherous waters and fast-flowing tides of her headlands and shore. Grenville, Drake, Frobisher, Fortescue, Hawkins, Chichester and Courtenay ... these names loom large on the roll of English naval history.

In this proud tradition the two major ports of Devon,

Plymouth (plates 70 and 71) and **Dartmouth (plates 74 and 75),** fiercely hold to the seafaring heritage of their past.

■ The southern coastline of Devon is strung with a line of white-walled hamlets abutting the rocky clifftop – as exemplified at **Bigbury-on-Sea (plate 72)** – which recede inland under a patchwork of fields shading green

under crop and showing reddish-brown under the plough. Waxing rich, this landscape provided tithes to raise the glorious cathedral at **Exeter (plate 73)** which possesses vast Norman towers on either flank and a richly-carved Western Front set within its Close.

(Overleaf: plates 74 and 75)

Close by the Devon border, where the River Tamar serves to denote the boundary between Cornwall and the rest of England, runs the biggest and most dramatic seascape walk in Britain. The coastal path commences at Mount Edgcumbe County Park in the south, runs westward to round **Land's End (plate 76)** and **Gwennap Head (plate 77)** and thence up the Atlantic seaboard to finish in the northeast at the summer playground of **Bude (plate 78)**.

Its course takes in the gentle beauty of the sand-flats at Hayle and the Fowey Estuary with its mild climate, woods and sub-tropical vegetation. It passes enchanting coves about the Lizard and **Pentire Head (plate 79)** where in spring the headland grass is carpeted with wild flowers – blue squills, primrose, bloody cranes bill, sea pink and mesembryanthemum – and the sheer cliff face becomes the nesting ground of shag and cormorant. However, for most of the South West Peninsula Coastal Path it is the rugged scenery which impresses itself upon the traveller – the ever-present sound of breaking ocean upon the shoreline, and the scream of gulls above the salt spray.

(Overleaf: plates 78 and 79)

Newquay (plates 80, 82 and 83) is the largest and most popular holiday resort in Cornwall. It lies midway between Land's End and Bude, on the county's northern coast. In former times it was merely a fishing hamlet whose houses huddled around the harbour, and was virtually unknown, save for its catches of pilchards. The fish came abundantly, but periodically, and it was the job of the huer – who occupied Huer's House on the headland just west of the harbour *(plate 82, right of centre)* – to watch for the shoals reddening the water, when, with a great shout he alerted the villagers.

The railway reached Newquay in 1875 with the intention of bringing china clay and tin to the port. The shallow waters of the harbour rendered this notion impracticable, and increasingly the trains brought in tourists. The town has subsequently grown up around the arc of its spacious, sandy bay and, within the last one hundred years, has extended in either direction along the craggy headland.

To the west of the town is **Towan Head (plate 81)**, which runs for nearly a mile out to sea and sweeps round, past its chaos of white water and rocks to the flat expanse of sand known as Fistral Bay.

(Overleaf: plates 82 and 83)

Cornwall's seafaring tradition has ensured that almost every village along its coastline has a harbour. Those of the larger towns are often extensive, as at **Penzance (plate 85),** which also boasts a floating dock, yet it is the very size of the smaller fishing villages, each grouped around its quay, that makes them so attractive.

At **Polperro (plate 86)** the harbour is but three acres in extent and dry at low tide – with so narrow an entrance that it is barred against winter storms by horizontal baulks of timber dropped one after the other into slots in the granite masonry. On the Camel Estuary, the ancient port of **Padstow (plate 84)** developed into a

shipbuilding port of some importance, but steam gradually replaced the old Padstow schooners. At **Mevagissey (plate 87)** fishing, and occasionally smuggling, were the main activities, and pilchards 'cured' in rock salt were exported as far afield as Italy and the West Indies. **(Overleaf: plates 86 and 87)**

St Ives (plates 88 and 89) has been a magnet for artists since the 1880s, when painters were lured here by the delights of its crisp, clear light. The best part of the town is on the neck of land between the harbour and the surfing beach of Porthmeor. The streets are narrow, and on either side of the steep alleys are galleries founded by the artist community. From Trencrom Hill three miles to the south, there are splendid views over the Hayle Estuary; west to the high haunts of prehistoric man and tinners, and south to **St Michael's Mount (plate 90).** This lofty, isolated mass of rock, some twenty-one acres in extent, is crowned by the most romantically sited of all medieval castles. At high water St Michael's Mount is separated from the mainland by a 500ft stretch of water, but at low tide a cobblestone causeway connects the two: this may be seen in the photograph as a very fine line running beneath the sea's surface. The mount has ever been a place of romance and mystery, having associations with Christ's legendary journey to Glastonbury. It lies at the terminus of a 'primary ley', aligned to the Mayday sunrise, which intersects, (without deviating from its course) the prehistoric monuments of Brent Tor, Cadbury Hill, Glastonbury and Avebury, as well as passing through the chancels of many churches dedicated to the dragon-killing St Michael and St George.

Plate 91: Coverack is a typical fishing village complete with stone-built, whitewashed cottages, a miniature harbour and a lifeboat station.

(Overleaf: plates 90 and 91)

By reason of their inaccessibility the Cornish coves of **Talland Bay (plate 92)** and **Cadgwith (plate 95)** are among the least known places in the Duchy. The former has been the scene of many wrecks, and the latter is reached down a narrow, winding lane which opens suddenly to the miniature cove. Cadgwith lies at the mouth of a well-wooded valley and its compact little

village of thatched, stone-built cottages – unspoilt by the march of time – is tucked neatly between high, rugged cliffs. Two small beaches are separated by 'The Todden', a diminutive headland leading to a secluded natural bathing pool hidden among the rocks.

The summer sun reflects on the wind-blown ripples of the Helford River at **Porth Navas (plate 94)** and upon

the wide ocean at the **Longships Lighthouse (plate 93)**. However, such tranquillity belies the true nature of the seas around the Cornish coast, and in severe storms waves have been known to lash the 110ft-high lantern of the Longships' light.

(Overleaf: plates 94 and 95)

The Isles of Scilly lie to the west of Cape Cornwall near the fabled lost-land of Lyonnesse. Of the cluster of islands, those of **St Martin's (plate 97)** and **St Mary's (plates 96 and 98)** – with Hugh Town as its capital – are the largest of the group. The seas around their shores are notoriously dangerous, and the cauldron of white water that surrounds the Isles' numerous reefs has proved the downfall of many a sailor. The worst recorded loss of life was that of *HMS Association* and four other ships that struck Gilstone reef in 1707. Over two thousand men were lost when the fleet foundered in raging seas, but its commander, Admiral Sir Cloudesley Shovel, was washed ashore at Porth Hillick Cove where, lore states, he was murdered for the sapphire ring on his finger by one of the island's wreckers. A rough stone monument marks the spot on the beach where his body was hastily concealed. **Mousehole (plate 99)** is a resort on the south coast of Cornwall. **(Overleaf: plates 98 and 99)**

No ancient town of England has preserved its medieval atmosphere to the same degree as **Wells (plate 100)** in Somerset. It takes as its centrepiece the soaring cathedral whose renowned West Front is the most ornate of any in the realm, and upon which is displayed the most extensive array of medieval sculpture to have survived the Reformation.

Wells possesses a fine example of a medieval close, surrounded by the houses of cathedral dignitaries. To the north lie the drum-like Chapter House and a row of lodgings built for the vicar's choral; to the south stand the cloisters and the partly rebuilt Bishop's Palace surrounded by its moat.

As if to mirror the spirit of Wells' Great West Front, the Elizabethan Manor House at **Montacute (plate 101)** exhibits carved statues of the Nine Worthies – Joshua, David, Judas, Maccabeus, Hector, Alexander, Julius Caesar, Arthur, Charlemagne and Godfrey de Bouillon – within Ham stone niches on its eastern face.

The city of **Bath (plates 102, 103 and 104)** includes at its precious Georgian heart the grandiloquence of the Palladian theme expressed to perfection in the curving terrace of John Wood the Younger's monumental Royal Circus and Crescent *(seen from the north, plate 102; and from the south, plate 104)*. Bath is the most elegant city in England, made famous by its Roman history and fashionable by the dandy, Beau Nash, in the 18th century.

A Romano-British settlement grew up around the spa, known as *Aquae Sulis* (the waters of the Celtic god *Sul*) and there was a temple dedicated to *Sulis Minerva*. The baths are among the city's main attractions, and a Roman reservoir beneath the Pump Room provides half a million gallons of mineral water a day at a constant temperature of 49° C, which still courses through a lead conduit laid down some 2,000 years ago. The Pump Room stands before the West Face of Bath Abbey *(plate 103, centre left)* which was raised in 1499 by Bishop Oliver King and occupies the site of the original foundation in which the first coronation of a King of all England – that of the Saxon king, Edgar – took place. Here, in 973, he took the threefold oath: *'To guard the church of God; to forbid Violence and Wrong; and to keep Justice, Judgement and Mercy'*. Thus has the oath persisted, unaltered, for over a thousand years.

Bristol (plates 106 and 107) has been a port for eight hundred years, importing wine from the Angevin territory of Bordeaux and from Spain since the Middle Ages, and has traded with the New World since the 17th century. The city's medieval churches speak of its prosperity, and foremost among them is St Mary Redcliffe *(plate 106, right foreground)* – one of the largest parish churches in the country. It is richly decorated and its massive tower bears a 285ft spire. The city's impressive 18th-century Corn Exchange, which can be glimpsed from the Redcliffe Heights, still displays the original nails upon which merchants once put their payment – from this custom originates the phrase 'to pay cash on the nail'. Scanning the Bristol horizon to the east, the heavy limestone pylons of **Clifton Suspension Bridge (plate 105)** come into view. Built by Isambard Kingdom Brunel in 1864, the structure is a powerful example of the enhancement of Nature by a man-made addition.

(Overleaf: plates 106 and 107)

Gerald Manley Hopkins saw Gloucestershire as a *'landscape plotted and pierced, of fold, fallow and plow'*. It is, like the Gaul of old, divided into three parts: the country of the hill, the country of the valley and the country of the forest – three parallel divisions extending from north to south. The first zone comprises the Cotswold Hills and the plateau which falls away from the escarpment to the east. Here stand clustered farming villages such as **Bourton-on-the-Water (plate 108)**, raised in local stone, its plan dictated by the River Windrush which flows through the village and is crossed at intervals by miniature stone bridges. The second division is that charming land of field and pasture which lies between the high ridges of the Cotswolds and the basin of the Severn. The last, and most diversified of all, contains everything to the west of the great river, including the Forest of Dean and numerous fragments of ancient coppice.

The vale of the Severn is a gracious countryside with a red soil merging into black, where wheat flourishes and cattle pastures and meadows **(plate 110)** are blessed with heaven's bounty. Within this valley the Severn is a river of infinite delights; little more than a wide stream as it flows through **Tewkesbury (plate 109)**, yet ever widening as it advances southwards to merge with the Wye and the **Bristol Channel (plate 111)**.

(Overleaf: plates 110 and 111)

Perhaps the greatest glory of **Tewkesbury Abbey (plate 112)** is to be found not in its architecture but in the golden, mellow stone of its fabric. This impression is also evident in the beautiful, unspoilt towns and villages of the Cotswolds. Typical of their number is **Chipping Campden (plate 113)** whose buildings – notably the 14th-century Grevel House, the Stuart Market Hall and the impressive Perpendicular Wool Church with its 120ft tower – seem shot with a honeyed appearance that is both restful to the eye and uplifting to the spirit.

■ The random course of the Wye is the most tortuous of all Britain's rivers, and its meandering forms graceful loops and horseshoe bends – as at **Ross-on-Wye (plate 115)** and, to an even greater extent, near its mouth **(plate 114)**. **(Overleaf: plates 114 and 115)**

From the air the county of
Worcestershire appears as a
great basin, open to the
south, but surrounded on its
other three sides by prominent
ranges of hills. The most
spectacular of these ranges
are the **Malvern Hills (plates
116 and 118)** – the 'true'
boundary between England and
Wales – which rise abruptly
from the chessboard pattern on
the hedge-fringed fields of
the lowlands, through skirting
woodland, to the furze and
bracken-covered heights that
are nearly 1,400ft above sea
level. From the beacon above
Great Malvern (plate 117) the
prospect is eastward over half
the Midlands and westward over
the domes and pinnacles of the
Welsh hills, to the Wye Valley
and the Black Mountains near
Brecon.
The Malvern range has a trench
running along the nine-mile
length of its summit (well
defined by an aerial
photograph) which formed an
ancient boundary line, and
still marks the county border.

The cathedral of **Worcester
(plate 119)** is, as it were,
the coping stone that adds yet
greater distinction to a very
distinguished shire. In this
splendid edifice is
represented every style of
church architecture from
early-Norman to the
Perpendicular. The crypt is
solidly Romanesque, the choir
has all the grace that the
early 13th century could
contrive and the nave clearly
belongs to the florid
Decorated style. To the late
15th century is ascribed the
fan-vaulted chantry chapel
raised above the tomb of
Prince Arthur.

(Overleaf: plates 118 and 119)

With the exception of London, Warwickshire probably receives more visitors than any other county in England. This is due not only to its scenic attractions but also to its historical associations. A mere list of names – Warwick, Kenilworth, Coventry, Rugby and Stratford-upon-Avon – conjure up visions from the past. Understandably, the greatest of these concerns Shakespeare, and the Bard's association with his native **Stratford-upon-Avon (plates 122 and 123)** has turned the sleepy dormitory town into a centre of 20th-century pilgrimage.

There are ghosts to be summoned at Rugby too – both factual and fictional – which dwell in the great, rambling pile of **Rugby School (plate 120)**. The architecture of four centuries is reflected in its varied walls, and it is neither difficult to hark back in one's imagination to the time of Dr Arnold and *Tom Brown's Schooldays*, nor hard to visualize the emergence of Rugby Football as a game when, in 1823, a young schoolboy, William Webb Ellis, *'with a fine disregard of the rules of football as played in his time first took the ball in his arms and ran with it.'*

Plate 121: Birmingham city centre.

(Overleaf: plates 122 and 123)

'The fairest monument of ancient and chivalrous splendour' was Scott's description of **Warwick Castle (plate 125)**, the gaunt stronghold of the Beauchamp Earls of Warwick, the foundations of which were first laid by Earl Turchil in the days of the Norman Conquest. The castle is one of the finest medieval fortresses in Europe

and its battlemented curtain walls and towers – chiefly of the 14th century – perch on a crag above the River Avon. Its principal entrance faces the town – down Gate Street to the church of St Mary whose incomparable Beauchamp Chapel houses the tombs of the castle's medieval custodians.

Capability Brown landscaped the castle grounds in the mid-18th century and it was he who was also responsible for laying out the 500 acres of parklands in which **Ragley Hall (plate 134)** is set. The fine country mansion was begun in 1680, with a portico and interiors designed by James Wyatt a century later.

Coventry (plate 126 and 127)
is often regarded purely as a
manufacturing city, yet it is
a place of great antiquity
which has lost few of its
intriguing corners in the face
of industrial development. It
was a thriving town when Earl
Leofric and his wife Godiva
founded its Saxon monastery in
1043. No account of the
city can ignore the legend of
Godiva who, it is said, rode
naked through the town,
modesty preserved only by the
length of her hair, in order
to obtain relief for the
people of Coventry from the
taxes levied by her husband.
Owing much to its central
location in the West Midlands
and its excellent
communications is Coventry,
the mechanization of whose
19th-century industries –
such as the manufacture of
bicycles and sewing machines
– contributed to its
prosperity and saw its
population increase sixfold.
The Daimler Company produced
Britain's first motor cars
here in 1898 and the car
industry developed rapidly,
giving rise in its turn to
munitions and aircraft
factories. The city was thus
an obvious target for
Luftwaffe bombers during the
Second World War, and in
November 1940 it was nearly
reduced to rubble by one
devastating enemy air raid.
The cathedral church of St
Michael, the city's proud
heart, was completely
destroyed save for its
medieval, flame-scarred tower
and blackened spire. The
cathedral's reconstruction in
Sir Basil Spence's
startlingly-modern style
(plate 126, centre), against
the charred walls of the old
cathedral, shows great
inspiration.

The countryside of Wales is possessed of a power and impressiveness – an elegance of spirit – that rivals anything that the rest of Britain can offer. Such is the landscape of the sinuous **Rheidol Valley (plate 131)** in Dyfed and of the nearby vale which brings the river to St Bride's Bay at the lovely coastal village of **Solva (plate 129)**. Less than a mile to the west, in the valley of the River Alun, is **St David's (plate 128)** – the shrine of the patron saint of Wales and one of the four Welsh cathedrals. Here, St David became Bishop of *Menevia* (the town's old name) after establishing a monastery and visiting Jerusalem. The existing cathedral is said to be the fourth on the site and near its western front can be seen the Bishop's Palace – built by Bishop Gower c1340 and the most splendid building of its type to survive anywhere in the British Isles. The same local purple stone of the cathedral was used with white stone in a chequerboard pattern in the Palace's Great Hall and its chapel. **Plate 130: the Claerwen Dam**, in the Elan Valley.
(Overleaf: plates 130 and 131)

Cardiff (plates 133 and 135) has grown, in little more than 150 years, from a sizeable village to become the capital of the Principality of Wales, a major seaport and university city. Utilitarian in parts, though not depressingly so, Cardiff displays that mixture of dignity and pragmatism that one would expect of the cultural centre of Wales. The circular keep of **Cardiff Castle** **(plate 134)** has surmounted its motte since Norman times, but the city's massive expansion at the turn of the present century resulted in the town becoming the world's principal coal port, and much of Cardiff's present-day appearance – particularly around the civic centre of Cathays Park *(plate 133)*, where stands the City Hall and County Hall, the University College and the National Museum of Wales – can be directly attributed to the Victorian and Edwardian eras. Dating from the same period is the famous rugby ground, **Cardiff Arms Park (plate 132)**, where beer and brawn are an integral part of the Welsh sporting ritual.

(Overleaf: plates 134 and 135)

The area due northwest of the Welsh capital, **the Rhondda Valley (plates 138 and 139)** is the heartland of Welsh mining and, to a very large extent, the coal from its pits is the reason for Cardiff's meteoric rise to prominence in the 19th century. The photographs looking northwestward towards Tonypandy *(plate 138)* and Ystrad *(plate 139)* show the way in which the urban sprawl has grown up along the line of the Rhondda; at first gripping the river's course, then slowly receding towards the moor-capped heights.

In ancient times, this area of the south formed the independent Welsh Kingdom of Deheubarth, but the gradual inroads made by Norman Marcher Lords extended English conquest from the mouth of the Wye as far west as Dyfed's Atlantic headland. Along this line of conquest runs a chain of castles – Monorbier, Carew, Chepstow, Llanstephan and Caerphilly – built to overawe the native population. The mightiest of them all, **Caerphilly Castle (plate 137)**, is one of the most splendid examples of military architecture in Wales. It was begun in 1271 by Gilbert de Clare and the castle's layout, when viewed from the air, is seen to be remarkably advanced; it bristles with ingenious details of internal defence, but its greatest triumph is the brilliantly-conceived water defences, designed to keep out of range the deadly military catapults which, at short distance, could batter down the most robust of castle walls.

Plate 136: Porthcawl Harbour, in Glamorgan.

(Overleaf: plates 138 and 139)

The town of **Pembroke (plate 141)** is built on a ridge which culminates in a great mass of limestone rock. Upon this rock was built **Pembroke Castle (plate 140)**, a key fortress in the Norman settlement of Wales. In 1457 Henry Tudor, Earl of Richmond, who as Henry VII became Britain's first Tudor monarch, was born at Pembroke and his special attachment to the town led to its close associations with royalty. Despite its links with the Crown Pembroke declared for Cromwell in the Civil War – the only town in Wales to do so – but when the war was practically over the custodian of the castle, John Poyer, inexplicably changed sides and held out against his former friends. The garrison finally surrendered to the Lord Protector and the castle's three renegade leaders were condemned to death. As an act of clemency it was resolved to execute only one, and lots were drawn for the victim. On two papers was written *'Life Given by God'*; the third, left blank, fell to Poyer and he was shot.

(Overleaf: plates 142 and 143)

The abiding beauty of the Welsh landscape is to be found in her mountains and along her serrated coastline. The grace of mountain scenery is exemplified by the photographs of the **Cambrian Mountains (plate 143)** in Powys and those of the **Upper Neath Valley (plate 142)**, which are shown ablaze with golden bracken enfolded within the lustre of russet moorland. Here, the views are wide and the horizon far; the wind sweeps freely across a vastness given over to the song of the meadow pipit and the plaint of the 'peesweep'.

Along the coastline of the **Gwynedd Peninsula (plates 144 and 145)** the varying nature of its rocks carve the coast into deep bays. Here, the mountains of Snowdonia lose their intensity and the land falls away to the sea in gentle folds. Upon the cliff's edge gorse blooms and sea fowl come to breed in such numbers as sometimes to conceal the rocks, whilst on the sea-jutting farmland, sheep and cattle graze in green plots of pasture.

Tenby (plates 146 and 147) is a bright, clean-looking resort sited on a narrow limestone promontory on the western side of Carmarthen Bay. At the seaward end of the headland is the insular knoll of Castle Hill, with its ruins and lifeboat station, with St Catherine's Rock as a kind of 'annexe' *(plate 147 lower right)*. Upon the latter is an impressive fort, constructed to guard the approaches to Pembroke dockyard.

(Overleaf: plates 146 and 147)

Just as the south coast of Wales has its castles stretching from the Marches to the ocean boundary, so has North Wales a string of concentric Plantagenet fortresses – at Conway, Beaumaris, Rhuddlan, Caernarvon and Harlech – but these are of a quite different order. The former were as much baronial mansions as fortresses, whilst the latter, built by Edward I after his conquest of the Principality of North Wales, were massively-fortified bastions for the protection of royal troops against hostile, native Celts. Indeed, at **Conway (plate 148)** it was not only the castle that was protected from Welsh revolt, but also the medieval town.

■ At **Rhuddlan Castle (plate 149)** Edward I organised his administration of Wales, secure behind its massive twin gatehouses and curtain walls enclosed by a moat. However, of all the King's military constructions, it is **Harlech Castle (plate 150)** that has the most impressive setting.

■ **Plate 151: Porthmadog Harbour**, in Gwynedd.

(Overleaf: plates 150 and 151)

Under the yoke of Plantagenet kings the flower of Celtic independence retreated into the fastness of the Snowdonia landscape, with its vast mountains, notched in places like battlemented towers, high passes and craggy peaks – like the summit of **Tryfan (plate 153)** – whence the spirit of Welsh freedom occasionally resurfaced in the guise of her hero princes: Llyweln the Great, Llywelyn ap Gruffydd and Owain Glyndwr. Some part of this essence of defiance seems to linger in these wild northern mountains, where deep, rock-girt cwms are bejewelled with gleaming tarns, such as Llyn Llydaw in **The Snowdon Horseshoe (plate 152)**. There is an all-pervading silence here, save for the bleat of lambs, the sudden flight of snipe, or the solitary call of the rare red kite – described by one native as *'the living flame of the sky'*. Soaring above all – dominating all – is the ethereal mass of Snowdon, the focus of bardic song and sentiment throughout the ages.

There is majesty, also, at the sea's edge – where the cold, green swell of the Atlantic ceaselessly breaks against the tiny islet of **South Stack (plate 155)** – with its lighthouse of 1809 – and in the sapphire seas to the west of **Solva (plate 154)**, whose unpredictable moods have lured many ships to grief on its shores.

(Previous pages: plates 152 and 153. Overleaf: plates 156 and 157)

Well demonstrating the influence that man can have upon the face of the landscape are the oil terminals at **Milford Haven (plate 158)**, which are the largest of their kind in Britain, and Sir Clough William-Ellis' Mediterranean fantasy of **Portmeirion (plate 159)**. The one dominates the scene and oppresses the sensibilities, whilst the other seems to exalt the spirit.

Angelsey is connected to the mainland by two famous bridges: Robert Stephenson's Britannia Bridge carrying the railway, and Thomas Telford's **Menai Suspension Bridge (plate 161)**, which has carried the road from London to Holyhead since 1826. Telford's bridge is his most famous and influential work, and is of cast iron supported by sixteen wrought-iron chains passing over tall masonry towers on either bank and anchored below ground. A similarly courageous engineering feat led to the construction of **Holyhead Harbour (plate 160)** whose Refuge – a one-and-a-half-mile-long, solid masonry breakwater – is the result of twenty-eight years incessant labour. The port is, today, a major terminal for ferries to Ireland.

Aberystwyth (plates 156 and 157) is a seat of governance as well as a holiday resort. The town grew to real importance with the establishment of its Norman castle *(plate 157, top left)* by Edmund Crouchback in 1277 It is still a place of significance, and opposite the ruins is a Victorian hotel bought a century ago to form the nucleus of the University of Wales.

(Overleaf: plates 160 and 161)

Returning across country to Essex – the most generous and least ambitious ot all the Home Counties – the landscape is seen from above as a chessboard of trim fields divided by straight hedgerows, and picked out with coppice and woods which show a deeper green against the prevailing tints of grass and the lovely sight of growing summer wheat. Within this mellow and fruitful landscape **Finchingfield (plate 163)** is the finest of the picturesque villages. Its duckpond (at the very centre of Finchingfield, where four roads meet) fed by the River Pant; its Georgian white-painted cottages; its gabled, barge-board houses; its 15th-century guildhall and almshouses; its Church of St John the Baptist crowning the curve of the hill, all give the village an air of having just materialised from a children's storybook.

In the top northeastern corner of Essex, above the Naze, the port of **Harwich (plate 162)** – *with Shotley on the distant horizon* – shares the fate of many ports of departure in that it is neglected by those who visit it only to leave. Few know it as a tightly-planned medieval town with one of the earliest lighthouses in Britain – looking like an Eastern pagoda – and a subject, on more than one occasion, for the artist John Constable. Alongside, there is an odd reminder of the discipline of earlier days in the Naval Treadmill Crane. Parkeston, where the Continental ferries tie up, lies round a bay within the sheltered lee of the Harwich peninsula; a thin wedge of land abutting the confluence of the River Stour from Manningtree and the River Orwell from Ipswich.

Two of East Anglia's most influential ports are **Felixstowe (plate 164)** and **King's Lynn (plate 165).** The former occupies a sheltered position on the Suffolk coast, made fashionable by Edwardian society. Today, its docklands are an important tanker and car-ferry terminal.

At King's Lynn, in neighbouring Norfolk, modern wharves jostle with the warehouses of Hanseatic traders and wool staplers for quayside frontage. At their backs stands the old town with its two guildhalls – both notable survivors of the early-15th century – each displaying striking flint chequerwork design. The bigger of the two is the largest medieval guildhall extant, and is now used as a theatre. Some six miles to the north of King's Lynn is the private country residence of the Royal Family: **Sandringham House (plates 166 and 167).** It was built by Edward VII, when Prince of Wales, in 1867-70 and comprises a seven thousand-acre estate, embracing the woodland and farmsteads of no less than seven parishes.

(Overleaf: plates 166 and 167)

The best way to view **Norwich
(plates 168 and 169)** is to
look down upon it, either from
the air, or as George Borrow
loved to look down, from the
heights of Mousehold Heath. It
is still a rural capital; a
medieval town which is really
an amalgam of villages
clinging to their old country
names – St Miles Coslany, St
John's Timberhill, St
Clement's-at-the-Fye-Bridge,
St James-in-Pockthorpe – each
clustered about its parish
church (of which Norwich has
more than any other city north
of the Alps), and at the
parochial centre rises the
marvellous cathedral set amid
the calm, though somewhat
commercial, oasis of the
Close.

To travel northwestwards from
the Norfolk capital is to
traverse a landscape of
settled fields draining into
dykes, rivers and immense,
unhampered skylines. Here are
found the splendours of
Houghton and **Holkham Hall
(plate 171)** set in their great
parks. Here and there lie
smaller, well-wooded estates,
and every mile or so brick and
flint cottages clustered into
a village, or set in groups
around some great medieval
ruin, as at Castle Rising.
The earthworks at **Castle
Rising (plate 170)**, upon which
the Norman motte and bailey
castle was superimposed, are
some of the most spectacular
in England and their scale can
only fully be appreciated from
the air. The site has yet to
be excavated in full and,
although the smaller
enclosures to the east and
west suggest a Roman
influence, the origins of the
main earthworks remain
uncertain.

(Overleaf: plates 170 and 171)

In Cambridge and Ely the
county of Cambridgeshire has
two of the most historic
cities in Britain. Each is
master of the landscape it
commands. In the north of the
shire **Ely (plates 172 and 173)**
has a cathedral whose soaring
western tower and octagon are
visible for miles around, its
stonework and white roof
shining out against the dark,
alluvial soil of the Fens,
across wide fields of sweet
grazing and root crops, where
dykes cut as straight as the
flight of an arrow.

In the south of the county
Cambridge (plates 174 and 175)
is held within a softening
landscape of rolling chalk
hills watered by tiny streams.
The town is often compared to
Oxford, yet the two have few
similarities and depend for
their beauty on quite
different circumstances.
Oxford is a great city in
which the university buildings
stand out from the banality of
much of the town. Cambridge,
on the other hand, is a small
city in which the university
buildings and churches seem to
form the greater part. Among
its treasures are the ancient
brickwork of Magdalene College
(a reminder of the former
Benedictine hostel); the
varied architecture and
quadrangles of Trinity
College; the old court of
Corpus Christi; the modern
chapel of Pembroke College,
built to the design of Sir
Christopher Wren; the 17th-
century chapel of Peterhouse
and, supreme above all others,
the Perpendicular chapel of
**King's College Cambridge
(plate 174, centre)** with its
fan-vaulted ceiling, and
elegant lawns running down to
the willow-shrouded banks of
the Cam.

(Overleaf: plates 174 and 175)

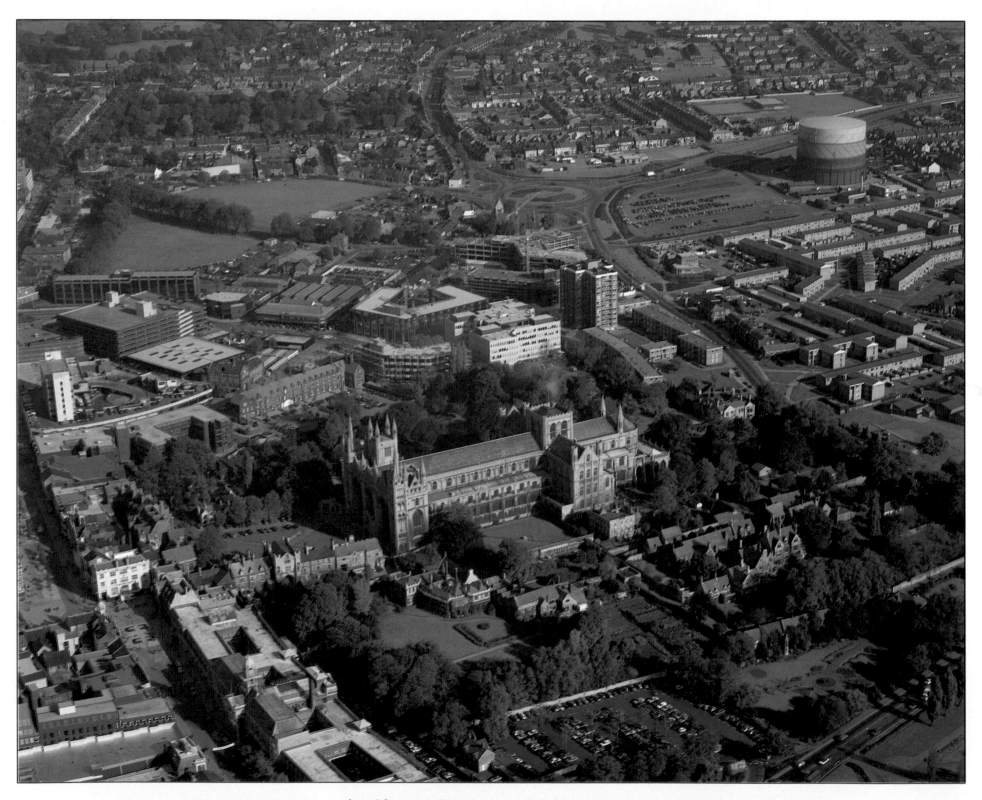

The ancient River Nene town of **Peterborough (plates 176 and 177)** originally grew up around a Benedictine monastery founded by King Penda of Mercia after his conversion to Christianity in 655. Within its shadow, the medieval town prospered and Peterborough achieved city status in 1541 when Henry VIII had the monks ejected from their Romanesque abbey and established the magnificent Barnack-stone buildings as a cathedral church. Among the domestic buildings of the monastery a few survive, particularly the Abbot's Palace, the Prior's Lodgings and the Knight's Gateway.

As well as being a sizeable market town and, since 1874, a municipal borough, the arrival of the railway and the advent of the Fletton brickfields stimulated Peterborough into becoming a thriving industrial centre that later embraced the processing of sugar beet grown on farms in the outlying countryside.

No one looking at the view of Lincoln (plates 178, 179, 180 and 181) can fail to be struck by the dominant position of the cathedral on its high ridge above the town and encircling fenlands of the Witham Valley. Here, in a materialistic and fragmented age, it testifies to the unifying spiritual belief in the Lord which, at the time of its construction, gave meaning and proportion to every aspect of life. The exquisitely pale colour – almost a shimmering silver haze – of the beautiful Ancaster and Lincoln limestone in which the cathedral is raised is a splendid foil to the pantiles of the secular buildings which huddle around its massive bulk; reminders of the trading connections between England and Flanders which first brought pantile roofing to the eastern districts during the 17th century.

The open space below the cathedral, known as Minster Yard, is full of interest. It was the site, in the Roman town of *Lindum Colonia*, of the great colonnade. Abutting the cathedral's Great West Front – whose tremendous breadth and elaboration is similar to the facades of Italian Renaissance churches – is the 14th-century Exchequer Gate, the largest of the gates in the encircling city wall, built soon after 1285 when the cathedral was granted a licence to fortify its precincts. Within this enclosure are still to be seen a fine tithe barn of c1440 and the ancient, Bishop's Palace.

(Overleaf: plates 180 and 181)

Boston (plate 182) stands slightly inland from the sea and is connected to the grey waters of the Wash by the River Witham as it flows down through the Great Lincolnshire Levels. By 1204, when King John granted a charter to Boston, its fame as a port was second only to that of London, and by the end of the 13th century it was paying more than the capital in customs duties. The great church at its heart, St Botolph's, is one of the largest and, in some respects, the grandest of all the parish churches of England; an expression of medieval civic pride, financed by the munificence of a Bostonian merchant class growing rich from the wool trade with the Hanseatic cities of Antwerp and Bruges. Almost entirely 14th century, it is an unrivalled example of late-Decorated architecture, whose lantern surmounts the loftiest church tower in the realm (the famous 'stump') to scan mile upon mile of flat fenland countryside divided into long, straight fields of multiple colours *(plate 183)*. Plagues, floods and the turning of trade towards new lands across the Atlantic led to Boston's decline as a major port, and the city has long since settled down to a quiet, though industrious, existence. There is, however, a wealth of charm still to be found in the narrow, winding streets which lead down to the quayside, where a steady, if somewhat meagre, business is still transacted upon the high seas.

The hand of man dominates the landscape of **Brampton (plate 184)** in Nottinghamshire, where the colossal form of its power station coolers sends forth dramatic columns of pallid vapour. At the Humber Estuary, however, man's influence, although of the same magnitude as at Brampton, is far more subdued. Indeed, the **Humber Bridge (plate 185)** – the longest of its kind in the world – could almost be described as a work of art as well as a mammoth work of engineering. The elegance of the bridge lies in its economy of construction; it seems to float over the river, upheld only by an arc of wire slung from its terminal piers.

Moving across country to Cheshire, there is no more striking sight from the air than the maze-like network of lines created at **Crewe (plate 186)** by the railway. No town is more obviously a 'railway town' and, after the land was purchased by the Grand Junction Company, its population increased from two hundred in 1841 to eighteen thousand within thirty years. At **Chester (plate 187)**, where local red sandstone gives the city its distinctive hue, the town's roots lie deeper in the past. The Romans knew the city as *Deva* and, in the Middle Ages, it was completely encircled by a two-mile stretch of walling still extant. Chester's famous half-timbered houses, known as 'The Rows', also date from medieval times, and are unique in Europe today.

(Overleaf: plates 186 and 187)

Positioned within the lovely moorland countryside of the Peaks, the spa town of **Buxton (plate 188)** is the highest in the kingdom. It is sheltered by hills even higher than its 1,007ft site, yet is able to offer gentle scenery more typical of the lowlands alongside sedate reaches of the lovely River Wye. **Ladybower Reservoir (plate 189)** is one such spot; where the russet of the bracken-covered limestone peaks is relieved by milder shades of green in the vale below.

The town itself is built around the thermal and chalybeate spring whose medicinal properties were exploited to the benefit of the town towards the end of the 18th century, when Buxton rivalled the elegant supremacy of Bath. The pale blue waters bubble up from a mile underground at the rate of a quarter of a million gallons a day. The town's architectural development was largely at the instigation of the 5th Duke of Devonshire, who built the beautiful Crescent, the Pump Rooms and the Devonshire Royal Hospital.

Within the borders of Yorkshire, now three counties, is a wealth of outstanding and diversified beauty; of bleak gritstone fells thrown into contrast against long, lovely dales; of colliery towns – that feed the power stations of Drax, Eggborough and **Ferrybridge (plate 190)** – contrasting with the medieval heritage of **York (plate 191)**, Beverley and Selby. The former has at its heart that *'jewel of light and glass'*, the High Minster of York; whilst **Selby (plate 193)** in North Yorkshire has a Benedictine Abbey of no less renown. The Minster at **Beverley (plate 192)** is still very much the focal point of the East Riding (although now officially incorporated in Humberside) and is one of the finest Gothic churches in Europe. Less than a mile to the northwest, along Beverley's main street, is the Church of St Mary *(page 192 centre, top)* which challenges St Mary Redcliffe and Boston for the accolade of finest parish church in England. **(Overleaf: plates 192 and 193)**

The southern corner of what used to be Northumberland is a tangle of heavy engineering, ship-building and coal mining: a conurbation now designated Tyne and Wear. Sullen and soiled, it still contains Britain's finest industrial city – the former provincial capital, **Newcastle (plates 194 and 195)**.

Travelling north from Newcastle over the Roman wall, the scenery of the ancient Kingdom of Northumbria is wild and solitary. Following the broad tide-line of the dune-girt shore the Castle of **Bamburgh (plate 196)** is eventually reached. Here is the strongest of a chain of stone fortifications strung across the Scottish borderlands. Bamburgh Castle stands upon a 150ft precipice of black basalt, within reach of the icy salt spray of the North Sea breaking on the strand below, looking out across the sand and sea to the Celtic Holy Isles of Farne. No castle could look more imposing: the site has been used for defence since the first wooden fortifications were raised here in 547 by King Ida, and Bamburgh remained the seat of Northumbrian governance until the mid-8th century. The present red-sandstone keep, chapel, living quarters and enclosures for the garrison and for prisoners date from Norman times, but with some rebuilding during Henry III's reign. Besieged and badly damaged during the Wars of the Roses, it was eventually allowed to fall into decay – a state from which it was rescued in the 18th century by the munificence of Lord Crewe, Bishop of Durham.

Plate 197: South Shields and North Shields.

(Overleaf: plates 196 and 197)

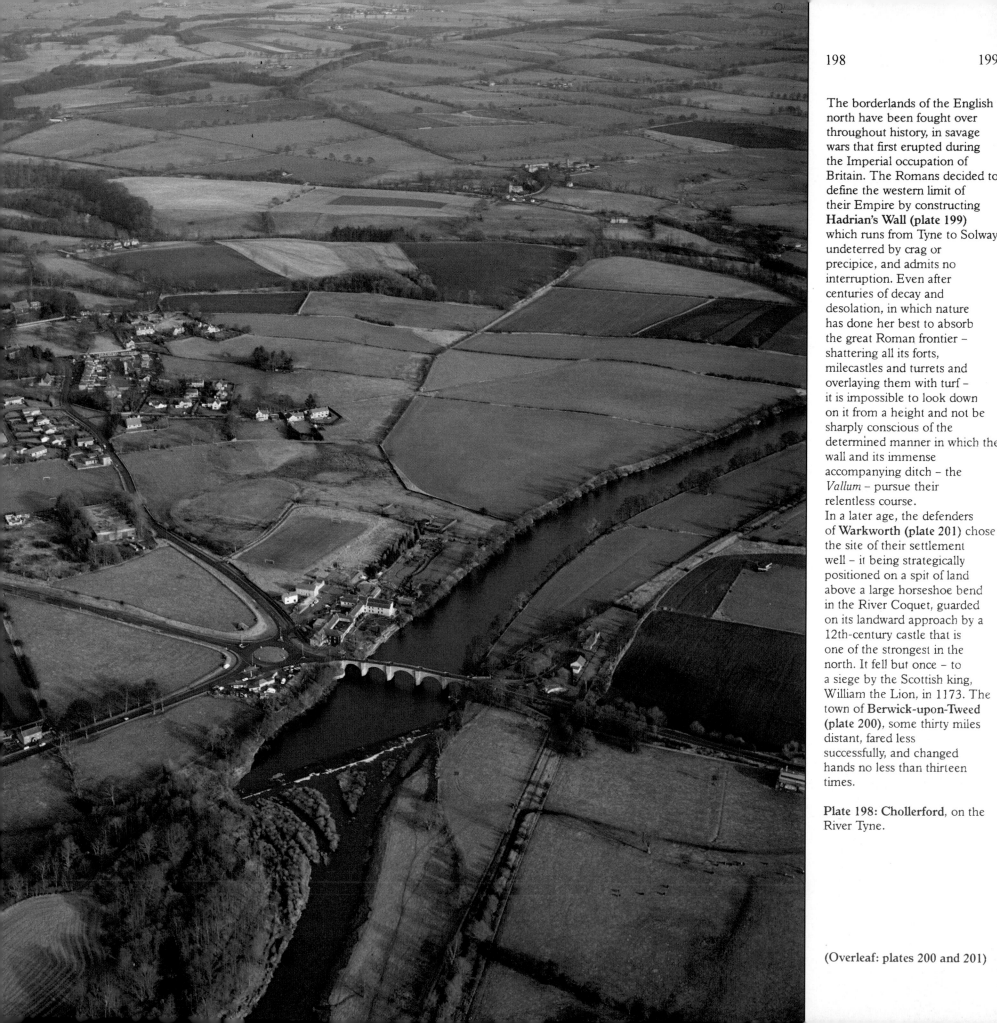

The borderlands of the English north have been fought over throughout history, in savage wars that first erupted during the Imperial occupation of Britain. The Romans decided to define the western limit of their Empire by constructing **Hadrian's Wall (plate 199)** which runs from Tyne to Solway undeterred by crag or precipice, and admits no interruption. Even after centuries of decay and desolation, in which nature has done her best to absorb the great Roman frontier – shattering all its forts, milecastles and turrets and overlaying them with turf – it is impossible to look down on it from a height and not be sharply conscious of the determined manner in which the wall and its immense accompanying ditch – the *Vallum* – pursue their relentless course.

In a later age, the defenders of **Warkworth (plate 201)** chose the site of their settlement well – it being strategically positioned on a spit of land above a large horseshoe bend in the River Coquet, guarded on its landward approach by a 12th-century castle that is one of the strongest in the north. It fell but once – to a siege by the Scottish king, William the Lion, in 1173. The town of **Berwick-upon-Tweed (plate 200)**, some thirty miles distant, fared less successfully, and changed hands no less than thirteen times.

Plate 198: Chollerford, on the River Tyne.

(Overleaf: plates 200 and 201)

Cumbria, comprising the old counties of Westmorland and Cumberland, is a land of misty mountains and placid lakes, possessing all the grandeur and concentrated beauty of configuration that one usually associates with the Alps. The region, known simply as the 'Lakes', lies at its heart and offers spectacular images of Wordsworth's poetry, where *'mountains against heaven's grave weight, Rise up, and grow to wondrous height'*. Here, the wild scent of bracken pervades the air and wafts down from mountain heights aglow with bright sienna tints – these areas of colour are particularly noticeable around the winter slopes arising from the shores of **Wast Water (plate 204)** and **Elter Water (plate 205)**. Geologically, the area is the domed uplift of the earth's crust, formed by volcanic activity which has exposed the oldest and hardest rocks at its centre – whence running water has cut dales which radiate from the mountain knot of the Scafell crests. Here the grandeur of the mountains and bold austerity of the rock crags are mirrored in the still waters of the area's lovely **Ullswater (plate 202)**, Ennerdale Water, Buttermere, Crummock Water and **Windermere (plate 203)** – each fed by the crystal streams and rivers of this, the rainiest region in England.

(Overleaf: plates 204 and 205)

Lakeland, filled with the souls of her poets, is a landscape where atmosphere paints its own unique images upon the scene. The glass-like reflections of the lakes themselves are the most enigmatic, where *'Nought wakens or disturbs their tranquil tides, Nought but the char that for the mayfly leaps and breaks the mirror of the circling*

deep'. The surfaces of lakes such as **Rydal Water** and **Grasmere (plate 209)**, **Derwent Water (plate 206)** and **Ullswater (plate 207)** possess a piercing turquoise sheen that is not a reflection of the sky, although it may be enhanced by it just as it is changed and patterned by every breath of wind.

One of the most spectacular lakes is **Buttermere (plate 208)** which lies like a stretched silken cloth below Great Gable. Here, with snow on the ancient volcanic rocks, and sculptured, marble-like cliffs gathered on all sides, it comes close to the primeval state of glacial desolation. **(Overleaf: plates 208 and 209)**

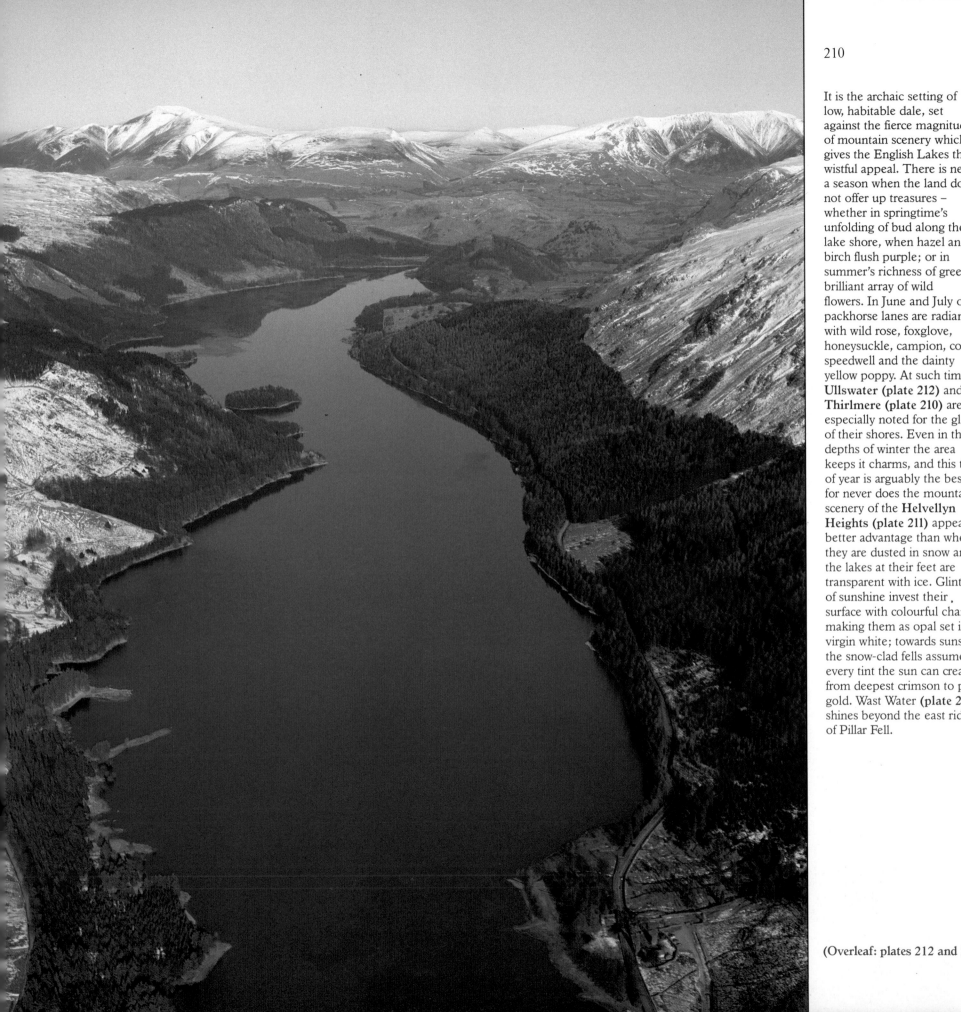

It is the archaic setting of low, habitable dale, set against the fierce magnitude of mountain scenery which gives the English Lakes their wistful appeal. There is never a season when the land does not offer up treasures – whether in springtime's unfolding of bud along the lake shore, when hazel and birch flush purple; or in summer's richness of green and brilliant array of wild flowers. In June and July old packhorse lanes are radiant with wild rose, foxglove, honeysuckle, campion, comfrey, speedwell and the dainty yellow poppy. At such times **Ullswater (plate 212)** and **Thirlmere (plate 210)** are especially noted for the glory of their shores. Even in the depths of winter the area keeps it charms, and this time of year is arguably the best, for never does the mountain scenery of the **Helvellyn Heights (plate 211)** appear to better advantage than when they are dusted in snow and the lakes at their feet are transparent with ice. Glints of sunshine invest their surface with colourful change, making them as opal set in virgin white; towards sunset the snow-clad fells assume every tint the sun can create, from deepest crimson to palest gold. Wast Water **(plate 213)** shines beyond the east ridge of Pillar Fell.

(Overleaf: plates 212 and 213)

Scotland possesses one of the most magical and yet one of the most terrifying landscapes. Her Highlands, as at **Ben Vorlich (plate 215)**, remain snow capped for much of the year; jagged friezes of mountain and moorland which, however imposing, are at certain seasons so hostile that their wilderness depresses rather than exalts the spirit. In the southern lands a softer, more poetic light informs scenes of a picturesque splendour with a strange and irrepressible charm – such as that which surrounds Sir Walter Scott's country house at **Abbotsford (plate 217)**. Indeed, the whole of the Lowlands seem touched by the spirit of the great author's historical romances, for the countryside appears everywhere to be dominated by its past and studded with medieval remains – of the bare skeletons of broken abbeys, like that at **Dryburgh (plate 216)**; and towering fortresses such as **Stirling (plate 214)** which looks out from its rocky pinnacle over the greatest field of Scottish valour; Bannockburn.

(Overleaf: plates 216 and 217)

A glance at the map of Scotland reveals how endlessly freshwater lochs stud the region, and how fantastically the coastline is indented by the sea – as at **Rhunahaorine Point (plate 219)** on Kintyre. Tortuous kyles and sea lochs add to the scenic effect, allowing the mysteries of the ocean to send their groping fingers amid the mountains, and to fumble along the tangle of golden weed that lines its shore – **Brodick (plate 218)** on the Isle of Arran.

Where the Lowlands run into the sea, there are high cliffs and remote beaches of white sand. Endless vistas of foam-flecked tides reveal at the foot of every other cleft in the sea-cliff a fine old fishing village with woods about it that might have been lifted directly from far East Anglia or the coastline of Freisia. It may be a place as big as Eyemouth or it might be small and quaint and a trifle bleak like St Abb's. It may be snug and pretty like **St Monance (plate 221)** in Fife, or large like neighbouring **Anstruther (plate 220).** Yet these fishing communities run to type, and that a rather distinguished type, born of the constant battle between man and the treacherous ocean with its fanged reefs, crosscurrents and sudden, violent storms.

(Overleaf: plates 220 and 221)

Culzean Castle (plate 223) stands on the Strathclyde coast, and is a typical product of the 18th-century Picturesque style – a building of Georgian symmetry and order, but with medieval trimmings. Swelling towers and turrets, battlements and machicolations are combined with sash windows and Robert Adam's characteristic arched recesses in his favoured Palladian tradition. Before its renovation the house was known simply as *'The Cove'*, but finding that a grandson of the first owner of the castle, John Kennedy, had styled himself *'Joannes Kennedy de Culzane'* in 1492, Adam's patron wrote it *'Culzean'* in the parish records, and 'Culzean' it became.

Ten miles out to sea from the castle is the domed granite rock of **Ailsa Craig (plate 222)** whose precipitous cliffs and fissures – thronged with screaming seabirds – perfectly conveys the atmosphere of the rugged coastline.

Dumfries (plates 224 and 225) is a Royal Burgh on the River Nith situated opposite its sister town of Maxwelltown on the far bank. The two are joined by five bridges which span the Nith, the oldest of which is a stone-built, six-arch structure. The town has had a stormy history ever since Robert the Bruce stabbed his nearest rival to the throne, the Red Comyn, in front of the high altar in Greyfriar's church in Dumfries. As a result, the noble houses of Scotland were thrown into disarray, whilst from the south came the army of Edward I with orders to suppress the claims of the Bruce mercilessly.

(Overleaf: plates 224 and 225)

At **Glen Etive (plate 226)** the low, winter light spangles the valley's many tarns and the thoughts of Wordsworth seem to carry in the frozen, still air *'... a silver current flows, with uncontrolled meanderings'*.

From above, the snowy landscape at **Loch Morlich (plate 227)** is monochrome and forbidding; the lake shimmers with light, and is highlighted against the shore's darkly-clad pine forests. The Cairngorms stretch away to distant peaks, marked here and there with a fan of scree thrown out by spasmodic torrents fashioned in the volcanic and glacial violence of their past. It is a cold and lonely place, assailed by driving rain; yet beauty, when it is to be found – perhaps in the play of cloud-shadows on the frozen slopes, or in the trail of mist across the moors – is, by its unsuspected nature, all the more enchanting.

(Overleaf: plates 228 and 229)

Scotland's two main cities are Glasgow, its oldest, and Edinburgh, its capital. The former was founded around AD 500 when St Mungo built his chapel by a ford on the River Clyde, a site now occupied by the Cathedral, parts of which date back to 1197. **Glasgow (plate 228)** has grown with enormous rapidity since the 17th century when its merchants set out to dominate the trade across the western seas. New World produce – cotton, sugar and tobacco – poured into the port, which in Victorian times became synonymous with Clydeside shipbuilding. This period of prosperity, which sought to satisfy the ever-expanding markets of the Empire, has given the city its Victorian character and has provided most of the city's municipal buildings and parks – Linn Park, Rouken Glen, Queen's Park and **Kelvingrove Park (plate 229)** in which the imposing Gothic fantasy of the Art Gallery and Museum *(plate 229, foreground)* is sited.

Edinburgh (plate 231) dates back to the early 7th century when King Edwin of Northumbria first established a settlement, but the city, although used as Scotland's capital by several monarchs in the 15th and 16th centuries, did not really establish itself until the Victorian era when the old and new towns first truly came together. Built upon hills, with higher peaks soaring behind it and the Firth of Forth at its feet, Edinburgh commands a dramatic location. From **Arthur's Seat (plate 231, foreground)** – its highest point – the whole panorama of the city can be seen and, far beyond, some twenty miles to the east, the famous light of **Bass Rock (plate 230)**.

Edinburgh Castle (plate 232), perched on a great volcanic outcrop of rock, overlooks the Old Town with its parallel thoroughfares of Hanover and Castle Street directing the eye past the Royal Circus to the distant quay of Granton Harbour on the Firth. The citadel so crowns the promontory that it is precipitous on three sides, and so well defended on the fourth that, throughout the centuries of medieval warfare, its summit remained inaccessible to attacking forces – save on two occasions – in 1296 when it fell to King Edward I of England, and forty-five years later, when it was recaptured by the Scots. Thus has the gaunt pile dominated the citizens of Edinburgh with an air at once threatening and protective; ready to assume either role, depending on the sympathies of its garrison.

Plate 233: the view over Edinburgh from Dean Bridge on the Queensferry Road, past the dome of the West Register House to the Salisbury Crags and the summit of Arthur's Seat.

*'Edina! Scotia's darling seat!
All hail thy palaces and
tow'rs...There Architecture's
noble pride Bids elegance and
splendour rise'.* Burns knew
the beautiful city of
Edinburgh well, and he is but
one of the many poets and
ballad-writers moved to praise
the Scottish capital; a city
through the streets of which
innumerable writers have
followed the history of an
ancient and romantic kingdom;
a city along whose flagstones,
wynds and closes pass the
ghosts of kings, queens and
princes. The street aptly
known as the **Royal Mile (plate
234)** connects the castle
stronghold with the
sovereign's 16th-century
Palace of **Holyroodhouse (plate
235, foreground)**.
Edinburgh's age of Georgian
elegance saw many fine
buildings erected – notably
Register House and buildings
in Charlotte Square by Robert
Adam; Thomas Hamilton's Royal
High School (modelled on the
Temple of Theseus, and adding
strength to Edinburgh's
nickname *Athens of the North*),
and many by James Craig. It is
the latter architect who is
generally regarded as the
founding influence for
Edinburgh's basic plan of
squares and broad
thoroughfares, and it is Craig
who must also take the credit
for building on one side of
Queen Street and Princes
Street only, leaving the other
side open as public gardens.

A short distance to the west of Edinburgh are the two great bridges of the Forth Estuary. The first to be built was the cantilever **Forth Bridge (plate 237)** which, at 2,765 yards long, was one of the great engineering feats of the 19th century. The photograph gives some idea of the impressive effect and stupendous scale of this graceful structure flung into the vast panorama across the shining expanse of the water. The bridge is used exclusively for railway traffic, while its rival, the **New Forth Bridge (plate 236)** is for road traffic.

■ Northwards, and over the Ochil Hills, lies **Perth (plate 239)** whose old town concentrates itself along the west bank of the River Tay. Three miles upstream is **Scone Palace (plate 238)**, an early-19th-century, castellated building occupying the site of the Coronation Abbey of Scottish kings. Here rested the legendary Tara – the Stone of Scone – until it was removed by the English and placed beneath the Coronation Chair in Westminster Abbey.

(Overleaf: plates 238 and 239)

The road and rail lines that span the Forth west of Edinburgh are carried across the Firth of Tay at **Dundee (plate 241)** by the graceful, two-mile-long, Victorian **Tay Railway Bridge (plate 240)** of 1887 and, eighty years its junior, the Tay Road Bridge which brings traffic right into the very heart of *'Scotland's Third City'*.

■ Where the Tay meets the North Sea, the headland of Fife sends golden fringes of sand around the coastline of the Ness; and it is here, on the northern shore, that the Royal Burgh of **St Andrews (plates 242 and 243)** stands. For many people the town spells nothing but golf – for its incomparable links make it the mecca of the

followers of the *Royal and Ancient Game*. St Andrews, however, is also the spiritual centre of Scotland – even though its cathedral now lies in ruins beside the quay *(plate 243, centre)* – and boasts the oldest university in the country.
(Overleaf: plates 242 and 243)

The soul of the Highlands lies in the heather-capped mountain heights above the ordinary haunts of men. The very names of some have a quality of godlike mystery and grandeur, even of terror – Stobinian, Lochnagar and dark **Schiehallion (plate 244)**. The latter rises for 3,547ft above Loch Rannoch, and is one of the best known landmarks in the Central Highlands. In contrast to this forest-shrouded land (given over to the raven and the deer) and the bare, bronzed moorscape of **Gleneagels (plate 245)**, the Border Region is a tableland of grassy hills and cool, green pasture – as witnessed in the **Eildon Hills (plate 246)**, and in the rich parkland and mature woods which surround Vanbrugh's **Floors Castle (plate 247)**; built in 1718 and later altered in the Tudor-style by Playfair about 1850.

(Overleaf: plates 246 and 247)

The Isles of the Western Coast possess a beauty which is all their own; an effect of light playing upon the sea. Near at hand the water is vivid blue, or even turquoise where the yellow of the shore changes the sea's hue, as seen at Baile Mor on St Columba's **Iona (plate 248)**. As the sea recedes so its very depth changes its colour to a deep violet, or an indigo sheen which serves to intensify the green of low isles like **Bute (plate 250)**, and throws into contrast the white sand bars of **Scaraster Bay (plate 249)** on South Harris.

Rothesay (plate 251) has given its name to the Prince of Wales' dukedom and, sited on sandy Rothesay Bay, it is the principal town of the Isle of Bute. The harbour is full of small craft in July, when the Clyde Yachting Fortnight is in full swing and steamers call at the pier. Nearby is Rothesay Castle which, when seen from above, stands out from the town as a green square with a moated fortress at its centre. There are four round towers linked by a curtain wall enclosing a circular courtyard and keep. The Normans stormed the castle in 1240, only to lose it some twenty-three years later to King Haco of Norway. The building was taken in turn by Robert the Bruce in the early 14th century.

(Overleaf: plates 250 and 251)

Loch Ness is one of a chain of lochs lying in the Great Glen, and extends from south of **Inverness (plate 253)** – popularly dubbed *'The Capital of the Highlands'* – to **Fort Augustus (plate 252)**, where the twin courses of the Caledonian Canal empty into the loch *(plate 252, lower centre)*. The waters of Loch Ness are darkened by peaty soil brought down to the loch by the numerous small burns and rivers that feed it. The murky depths are supposedly the haunt of its famous monster; stories of which stretch back to the 6th century (when St Columba prevented it from eating a Pict) and beyond, into the mist of Gaelic lore. which states that each *Visque* or *fearsome water-horse* inhabits every dark sheet of water in the Highlands.

■ **Pittenweem (plates 254 and 255)** in Fifeshire is a Royal Burgh which compounds a delightful scene of old, red-roofed houses grouped around its ancient fishing harbour. **(Overleaf: plates 254 and 255)**

Of Aberdeen's two rivers, the
Dee is more famous than the
Don, for it flows through the
open-hearted, gracious
landscape so beloved and
popularized by Queen Victoria.
Realizing that her heart was
in the Highlands, she resolved
to make a home at Balmoral.
The Prince Consort purchased
the estate in 1852 for £31,000
and had the old house (first
mentioned in 1484 and known as
Bouchmorale, which is
appropriately Gaelic for
majestic dwelling) rebuilt in
his own fantasised version of
the Scottish Baronial style.
The resultant chateau-like
mansion of **Balmoral Castle
(plates 256 and 257)** is rich
in 'fairy story' turrets and
gables and, lying on a large
sweeping curve of the River
Dee, is surrounded by pine
woods, heather moors and
sombre expanses of deer
forest.

Sited at the confluence of the
Rivers Leven and Clyde,
Dumbarton (plate 258) was once
the centre of the independent
Kingdom of Strathclyde, and
has a royal castle standing on
the majestic, 240ft-high
Dumbarton Rock *(plate 258,
centre)*. To the west is the
port of **Tarbert (plate 259)**,
the centre of the Loch Fyne
herring industry. It lies on
the tiny isthmus on the shores
of East Loch Tarbert – the
little neck of land linking
Knapdale with Kintyre. Magnus
Barefoot of Norway is said to
have been ceremonially dragged
by his warriors in a longship
from Tarbert across this
isthmus in 1093 – a distance
of nearly two miles.

(Overleaf: plates 258 and 259)

It does not take the road at **Glen Shee (plate 260)** long to rise out of its vale to the high country of the mountains. As at **Loch Tay (plate 261)** under a cloak of snow, it is not a comfortable scene that meets the eye, but one to marvel at in all its gaunt and threatening majesty.

At **Gigha Island (plate 262)** the view is westwards across the Sound of Jura to distant Islay. **Tobermory (plate 263)** 'The Well of Mary' is the chief town on the Island of Mull. It was founded in 1788 by the Society for the Encouragement of the British Fisheries, but failed to realise the hopes of its founders and has never been an

important fishing station. It stands on the shore of a bay in which one of the galleons of the Spanish Armada was blown up and sunk in 1588 by Donald Glas MacLean. **Plate 264: Blackpool**, with her two piers, famous 518ft tower and seven-mile-long promenade. **(Following pages: plates 262, 263 and 264)**